ROCKHOUNDING
Texas

A Guide to the State's Best Rockhounding Sites

MARTIN FREED AND RUTA VASKYS

ESSEX, CONNECTICUT

An imprint of Globe Pequot, the trade division of
The Rowman & Littlefield Publishing Group, Inc.
4501 Forbes Blvd., Ste. 200
Lanham, MD 20706
www.rowman.com

Falcon and FalconGuides are registered trademarks and Make Adventure Your Story is a trademark of The Rowman & Littlefield Publishing Group, Inc.

Distributed by NATIONAL BOOK NETWORK

Photos by Martin Freed and Ruta Vaskys unless otherwise noted
Maps by Melissa Baker, The Rowman & Littlefield Publishing Group, Inc.

British Library Cataloguing in Publication Information available

Library of Congress Cataloging-in-Publication Data
ISBN 978-1-4930-6753-4 (paper: alk. paper)
ISBN 978-1-4930-6754-1 (electronic)

♾™ The paper used in this publication meets the minimum requirements of American National Standard for Information Sciences—Permanence of Paper for Printed Library Materials, ANSI/NISO Z39.48-1992.

CONTENTS

INTRODUCTION

Between the two of us, we have almost 60 years of prospecting under our belts. We have scoured the landscape from Newfoundland to Alaska to Florida to southern Mexico and everywhere in between. Over the years, guidebooks have been a valuable tool; however, they have had their shortcomings. Often they are out of date. The author might have been to the location 30 years ago, and when the reader shows up at the site, they may find a subdivision on top of the agate bed. In addition, roads change, as do landmarks. Some guides indicate that they've been revised, but often the changes are just the addition of a few sites, while it is apparent that the author had not revisited the locations in the previous edition.

Another gripe that we have with some guidebooks is that they often build up the reader's expectations. They give a list of minerals that may be found, but many are rather scarce. We attempt to give the reader a realistic idea of what they may be able to find at each site by noting in the rockhounding description whether we found the materials ourselves or whether they have been reported by others. We often also state how much time we spent at a location and exactly how many pieces of each mineral we found.

Over the years we often complained about guidebooks. In fact, we griped so much that our rockhounding friends said, "Why don't you write your own book?" So here we are writing our second rockhounding book: *Rockhounding Texas*.

Texas Overview

Size

Texas is a vast state. It is over 800 miles from El Paso in the west to Texarkana in the east. And over 800 miles from the Oklahoma border in the Panhandle in the north to McAllen at the mouth of the Rio Grande in the south. The state encompasses over 275,000 square miles of land.

The name Texas was taken from a Native America language of the Caddo Indians who called the region Tejas. The name came from the Spanish spelling of the Caddo word *taysha*, which translates to "friend" or "ally." The original Spanish settlers knew the western Caddo peoples as "the great kingdom of

Tejas." The state flower is the bluebell, which grows in the fields of the central region resulting in a sky-blue coating that blends with the sky so that it is difficult to see where the horizon line is located. These flowers also produce a heady scent that seems to permeate the entire atmosphere. The state bird is the mockingbird, which is found statewide and can often be observed sitting in the pecan trees. The state rock is petrified palm wood, and the state gemstone is blue topaz.

Environmental Regimes

This vastness of the Lone Star State incorporates at least nine different classifications of environmental vegetative regimes. These are: the High Plains, Basins and Mountains of the Desert, the Hill Country and the Edwards Plateau, South Texas Brush Country, Piney Woods, Gulf Marshes and Prairies, Grand Prairie and Cross Timbers, Blackland Prairie, and Post Oak Belt. Each one of these environmental areas necessitates a different approach to our avocation of rockhounding.

Weather Zones

Besides size and environmental regimes, the Lone Star State sports an impressive array of weather zones. Winnie, Texas, east of Houston in the southeast part of the state receives an average of almost 60 inches of rain a year. Contrast this to the Trans Pecos Region, which includes El Paso, where the annual rainfall is about 15 inches a year.

Temperature and wind conditions also vary widely. In the Panhandle below zero Fahrenheit temperatures are common in the winter with windchills a lot lower. The flat interior regularly experiences hot summers where the thermometer soars to well over 100°F. In addition to the heat, along the south coast the humidity hovers near 100 percent sometimes for days at a time. This makes the environment even less hospitable.

Each of the above meteorological conditions offer different challenges to rock hounds.

Rockhounding Possibilities in the Lone Star State

In part because of its vastness, the state processes a great variety of treasures for rock hounds to seek out. However, the majority of the land is either private or parks. While this does inhibit rock hounds, the Lone Star State has tens of thousands of miles of public State of Texas roadways, over 71,000 in fact, and it is legal to collect along the shoulder of these rights-of-way. This offers a lot of opportunities to collect the vast variety of fossils, gemstones, and minerals found within the state.

Oil and gas dominate the mineral industry in the state. However, there are a number of other minerals that are also mined here. They include, but are not limited to, salt, silver, lead, magnesium, uranium, graphite, talc, iron ore, pink granite for building, and gypsum.

In the past there had been a number of "pay to rockhound" ranches and farms. Almost all of these have changed hands, or the folks became tired of business and do not allow it any longer. However, the status of these things changes over time, so it pays to check around if you care for this type of collecting.

HAZARDS AND PRECAUTIONS

Snakes

Although snakebite incidents are relatively rare when compared to the number of people roaming around Texas, anyone venturing into the wilderness should take certain precautions. Not all snakebites can be prevented, but a few simple steps will greatly reduce the risk:

- Know how to identify poisonous and nonvenomous species.
- Take a snakebite kit and become familiar with its use.
- Know where to go for help.
- Know the most common symptoms of a snakebite:
  -bloody discharge at wound site
  -fang marks
  -swelling at the site of the bite
  -severe localized pain and discoloration
  -swollen lymph nodes near the bite
  -diarrhea, burning, convulsions, fainting, and/or dizziness

The symptoms may resemble other medical conditions. Consult a physician if you think you've been bitten.

Treatment for snakebites: Stay calm and act quickly. Get help fast, but while waiting for assistance, do the following:

- Wash the bite with soap and water.
- Keep the bitten area lower than the heart.
- Apply a cool compress.
- Monitor breathing and heart rate.
- Remove all rings, watches, and constrictive clothing, in case of swelling.

If unable to get help within 30 minutes, the American Red Cross recommends the following:

- Apply a bandage, wrapped 2 to 4 inches above the bite, to help slow the venom. This should not cut off the flow of blood from a vein or artery—the band should be loose enough to slip a finger under it.

- A suction device can be placed over the bite to help draw venom out of the wound without making cuts. These devices are often included in commercial snakebite kits.

Prevention: Of course, it's best to prevent a snakebite to begin with. Take the following precautions:

- Do not harass any snake (or any other wildlife for that matter). Many bites occur as a result of someone trying to kill a snake or getting too close to it.
- Do not walk through tall grass unless absolutely necessary. Stick to the hiking paths as much as possible.

Always carry a snake stick and tussle the brush ahead of you.

- Watch where you put your hands and feet.
- Be especially cautious when rock climbing.

Most important, do not let a fear of snakes stop you from having a good time in the outdoors. Bites are very rare—just take some precautions.

Insects

The following critters are more annoying than snakes—and can be just as dangerous. Just a few simple precautions, however, can save the day.

Mosquitoes

These are the most common pests. In some areas of the state, especially the lowlands, they could carry diseases, some of which are life-threatening. However, they can be easily deterred by taking the following steps:

- Use a repellent. Many experts believe that the most effective are products that contain DEET. The higher the percentage of this ingredient, the better. If you do not want to use DEET, Natrapel works but perhaps not as well.
- Mosquitoes are most active around dusk. Staying indoors during this time will limit exposure.
- Cover as much of your skin as possible with clothing. Some people also wear head nets.

No-see-ums, or Gnats, and Other Biting Flies

If you ever have to spend a night dealing with these guys, it will be long remembered. Some call them sand fleas, as they are usually found in sandy or gravelly areas. They are small enough to pass through all but the finest screens, so make sure your tent or camper is so outfitted.

DEET works well on no-see-ums, and we have spread it on our screens with some success. Since these insects are attracted to light, it is best to do your reading before dark.

Bees

These guys can be a real hazard for some folks: those who can go into anaphylaxis shock. This is a very severe allergic reaction and can be life-threatening if not treated immediately. Even if you are not subject to this condition, a series of bee stings can be quite unpleasant to say the least.

A few simple precautions can prevent most of these interactions. Always be aware of where you are walking to. Rock hounds have a tendency to always be looking down and not ahead. That is not a very good idea. Stop and lift your head up and look around after a few steps. If you get stung, always remove the stinger as soon as possible, wash the wound with soap and water, and hold a piece of ice on the affected area. If needed, take an over-the-counter pain reliever; and if an arm or leg is affected, elevate it.

Arachnids

Ticks

Various species of ticks are found throughout Texas. A bite from an infected tick can result in a serious disease. Here are a few precautions:
- These guys hang on foliage, waiting for a host to walk by. Stay on rocky or sandy trails.
- Rub insect repellent on your legs.
- Wear your pants inside your socks and put repellent on them. White socks are best because the ticks will be easier to spot.
- Check your skin for ticks every evening, or have your partner do it for you.
- If you happen to get a tick bite, keep in mind that the longer the critter is attached, the more likely it is to pass a disease on to you. If you cannot get professional medical help quickly, take a good pair of

tweezers, grab your skin below the tick's mouth, and pull it off. Dab with alcohol and bandage.

Spiders

A few poisonous spiders inhabit Texas, but very few spider bites are reported. Folks usually get stung when they roll over onto the critter or try to scratch it as it is walking up their body. Stay aware of what is going on around you.

Scorpions

Many species of scorpions inhabit Texas. Most experts agree that there are not many medically dangerous scorpions in the Lone Star State. However there have been occasional reports of one that is dangerous to humans: *Centruroides exilicauda*. In any case, while found in good numbers in Arizona, they are quite scarce in the Texas. Though not fatal, a sting could cause great discomfort. So precautions are advised. The best way to protect yourself is to look at the bottom of every rock you pick up. Drop it immediately if a scorpion is present. Also, if you take off your boots, check them for scorpions and spiders before putting them back on.

Mammals

Bears

Black bears are relatively common in the mountainous and hill forests of Texas. These guys are very shy, and you should consider yourself lucky if you see one. However, a few precautions should be taken not so much to protect humans from bears, but the other way around. It's usually the carelessness of humans that produces a nuisance animal, and occasionally one has to be dispatched.

- Always keep your food in bear-proof containers.
- Keep your campsite clean and neat.
- Do not throw garbage into open receptacles. We've noticed that some areas in the western part of the state now have bear-proof garbage cans.
- Head in the opposite direction, very slowly, if you see a cub.

Cougars and Other Cats

While these large cats are generally scarce in most areas of Texas, they can be relatively abundant in mountainous places and in western Texas. If you are in higher-elevation forest, which could be mountain lion country, keep a close eye on children and pets. If attacked, act aggressively: pick up a big stick, throw rocks at it (not the agates you just picked up), and so on. The cat will almost always be intimidated and go find easier prey.

There are number of other species of large cats that are native to Texas. These include bobcats, jaguarundis, and ocelot. Except for the bobcat, these are rather scarce and do not pose a threat to humans. However, precautions should be taken to protect your pets: small dogs and cats. Keep them under control and within your vision at all times.

Other Mammals

While raccoons, possums, foxes, coyotes, jackrabbits, and other small mammals are not usually a threat, rabies could be a problem. This disease can make even the shyest critters aggressive. If you see any animal acting strangely, do not approach it. Move away.

Plants

Poison Ivy and Poison Oak

Most people are at least somewhat allergic to the oils produced by these two plants. The best way to protect yourself is to learn to identify them and make sure you are not exposed. Standard clothing does not help very much, since the oil can penetrate the fabric and reach your skin. In fact, you can develop the symptoms by touching the affected clothes after they are taken off. The oils can also be spread from person to person by touching.

In order not to ruin a trip, take an antihistamine salve along just in case someone develops the rash. A number of good ones can be bought over the counter at most pharmacies. If the condition is severe, seek medical help.

Cacti

Cacti may not be life-threatening but if you get into one badly, it surely will ruin your day. If the area has lots of these succulents, a few simple precautions can prevent a ruined day. Heavy pants or boots when practical will help. At times, leather gloves can be needed to prevent a sticker from penetrating your palm.

Carry pliers with you to pull the plant off if someone gets stuck. It is very frustrating when a cactus section is pulled off an area of skin only to reinsert itself into another part of you or a friend.

The Sun

The sun is very strong in Texas. If you are fair-skinned, be sure to include a good sunscreen in your supplies. It should have an SPF of at least 25. The best way to treat sunburn is to avoid it. However, if it happens, a number of over-the-counter remedies are available that can treat the discomfort and minimize the chance of infection.

Mild cases of sunburn can be treated by taking a cool shower or applying cold cloth compresses. The application of topical agents such as aloe vera and/ or salves containing hydrocortisone could be helpful. Severe sunburn should be treated by a medical professional. Do not wait until you get home—find a local doctor or even an emergency room if necessary.

The symptoms of sun poisoning are fever, nausea, vomiting, fatigue, dizziness, red skin rash, and/or chills. Seek medical help at once.

Boating

Occasionally people use boats to reach good rockhounding sites in Texas. Be aware of the boating regulations and what equipment is needed. Each vessel should be equipped with one personal flotation device (PFD) for each individual on board, in the appropriate sizes for kids and adults. Some boats require fire extinguishers, whistles, flares, and running lights. These things do get checked.

Abandoned Mines

Though there aren't too many opportunities for rock hounds to gain access to active or abandoned mines in Texas, if you are lucky enough to have the opportunity, some precautions must be taken. Be extra careful around abandoned mines. Vertical shafts may be overgrown with vegetation and not readily apparent.

Do not go into any mine shaft unless you know what you are doing and have backup help. Most old mines have lots of boards and trash lying around.

Look out for rusty nails and other sharp things protruding from wood. You can also get badly cut by stuff like old metal, glass, or even tailings. Be careful.

Back Road Driving

Though most of the sites listed in this book are on good highway, some are not, and if you pursue this avocation, sooner or later you will find yourself on a really terrible road heading uphill with a vertical drop-off on one side. Sure enough, you will meet a vehicle coming down the road and there are no pull-offs. What do you do? Remember that the vehicle going uphill has the right-of-way, as it is much more dangerous backing down than up. While driving down these one-lane roads, try to remember where the turnouts are so you will know how far you would have to back up if need be.

Some of these roads are rather steep. If you drive a big truck like us, when you reach a crest, you often cannot see the road over the hood. Do not assume that the tracks are straight ahead—the road could make a sharp turn. Either step out yourself or have a passenger get out to see where the path heads.

If the road ahead looks bad, do not continue driving. Get out and take a look. Remember that four-wheel drive is there to get you out of trouble, not into trouble.

Weather

Everyone knows that the southwestern desert gets very hot in the summer. If you are 10 miles into the backcountry and your vehicle breaks down, you'd better have enough water to hike out. Better yet, be sure your vehicle is in good shape before heading into the area. Also make sure you have enough fuel.

Certain parts of Texas can be very cold in the winter. Be prepared if you are heading into the mountains. The road could be cut off by a big snow-storm, so carry extra blankets or sleeping bags and food and water for such an occurrence.

Rainstorms are also dangerous, especially at high elevations. Lightning strikes can kill. If the weather is threatening, do not throw on your backpack and start up the trail. During wet periods many roads become impassable. Make sure the road is OK before heading out or, better yet, wait for dry weather.

Tornados do occur in most areas of the Lone Star State. Keep yourself aware of the weather forecast to know if these storms might be a problem on a particular day. We now have computer simulations for the occurrence of twisters. Avoid those areas on a particular day if that's the prediction.

Roadside Parking

This is the most important caution that we write about. Since most of the rockhounding in Texas is done in the right-of-way of roads, parking can be quite dangerous. Be very careful where you pull out. Make sure that other vehicles have plenty of room to pass.

We attempt to describe the best places to park, but you might have to walk a bit to get to the area. We know it is tempting to stop wherever you see a promising location, but remember it's better to take a little stroll than cause an accident, besides the fact that moving is good for you.

Trespassing

Texans are very serious about trespassing. So when roadside collecting, be sure to stay on the shoulders of the road. You do not want the sheriff to show up and drag you off to the jailhouse. They will probably spend a few hours making you sweat about whether they will prosecute or not. This does happen, so a word to the wise is sufficient.

WHERE YOU ARE ALLOWED AND NOT ALLOWED TO COLLECT

Collecting is not permitted in national parks, national monuments, and wilderness areas. You can get permission from private landowners to collect on their property; this takes time and effort for collecting locations, but their statuses are very fluid so we did not include them. If you are interested in this type of rockhounding, join a group like Texas Rockhounding on Facebook. Many members will point you in the right direction.

ROCKHOUNDING ETHICS

Mineral collecting is a fascinating and enjoyable avocation. We rock hounds have a code of ethics that must be followed to enable us to continue to enjoy our passion. Here are the self-imposed restrictions that we abide by:

- Never collect more than you can use. Leave some for the next group of rock hounds.
- When you dig holes, always fill them in.
- Do not leave big tire ruts that could cause additional erosion.
- Always be sure that you are collecting within the right-of-way on the road system or have permission.
- Carry out any trash you produce, and if you see anybody else's, consider picking that up too.
- Always leave gates as you found them. If they were open, leave them open. If they were closed, close them behind you.
- Be very careful when making campfires. The Southwest is generally very dry, making the brush extremely susceptible to fires. If you must build a campfire, make sure you do so in a well-made fire ring, and douse the fire completely afterward. Better yet, do your cooking on a small camp stove.

HOW TO USE THIS BOOK

The Plan

A few months before heading out to do the research for this book, because of the varying conditions and environment of the Lone Star State, it was obvious that a plan had to be hatched. We have been rockhounding Texas for a few decades. As a result many sites were known to us. However, there also are many more that were not. Our plan was to visit the known locations and explore the road system for a few miles around the area that we usually visit. That is, driving a few miles and making a stop where a pull-off is easy and safe. For the areas between our known locations, we drove 5 miles before stopping again and looking around. If some material of value was found, we made more stops close by.

We crisscrossed Texas for almost three months following our plan preceding the writing of this guidebook and made over 400 stops. Of the 400, 108 contained enough material to be worthy of a listing in the volume. Of the remaining, many held material, many did not, but none were worthwhile, in our opinion, of going out of your way to inspect. Of the 400, many were personally prospected by us over the years. Information about the others came from friends, rock hounds, Internet searches, and other sources. Most of the latter did not work out.

This book should be used not only as a guide to specific locations, but also as a general guide pointing to an area where the reader can then do their own prospecting. We found so many places by just making additional random stops.

GPS Coordinates

While it is not necessary to have a Global Positioning System (GPS) to find any of the areas described in this book, we give latitude and longitude readings for most of the sites. The GPS numbers were obtained using the Latitude Longitude Finder app on our Android cellphone. The positions are reported in degrees and decimal of degree. We noticed that different apps appear to calculate the positions differently. These are very minor and insignificant. Most carry out the numbers to seven or eight digits or beyond. The latitude number at the fifth digit to the right of the period changes only about 3.5 feet for each increment. For example, a latitude number of 31.19376 is only about 3.5 feet farther north than 31.19375. At the sixth digit the difference is about 4 inches. The longitude reading at these latitudes is almost the same but the calculation is a bit more complicated. The point is that slight differences in GPS numbers are really insignificant. In a few cases, good readings could not be taken exactly at the site and had to be moved slightly. Unless otherwise noted, the readings were taken at the site. If not, the best description of where they were obtained is given. When using other guidebooks, we found it frustrating not knowing whether we actually found the site described. The GPS coordinates can confirm that the reader did indeed find the correct location.

The elevations were obtained with the Android cellphone app GPS Altimeter. If you use a different app, there might be small discrepancies.

Accommodations

We are campers and over the years have stayed at many, if not most, Texas state parks. A bad experience was never encountered. The Lone Star State has an excellent park system. For each site, where possible, a close state park is listed. The type of campsites available are listed. We also note if there are other RV resorts and/or campgrounds in the area.

For those who prefer motel or hotel accommodations, we note where those may be found.

Special Attractions

Our approach to this book was to make it more than a rock collecting missive. Over the years, after meeting many rock hounds, we learned that most, but not all, had other interests. A prominent one was angling. In this book, for many locations, a favorite fishing hole in the area is described. We attempt to list the species available, techniques for catching them, and the best time of year where this information is available.

Other favorite activities are also noted: hiking, biking, wildlife and bird watching, and picnicking.

When out in the field, if an inclement weather day occurs, visiting a museum is a great distraction. And Texas is a great place to go museuming. Almost every county has at least one. These institutions have displays of local, state, and national history. Many have exhibits of the local rocks around their area as well as explanations of the natural history of the area.

Finding the Site

The mileages are given to tenths of a mile. This means that they may be off by almost two-tenths. This is really not all that important because almost all the sites extend for long distances on either side of the location. In some cases, the directions are given from two different approaches.

Rockhounding

Here's where we get into the meat of the situation. What can be found and how to look for it is described. Do you scrape or look around? In some cases, one method is superior to the other. Also, where large items are encountered, we discuss the use of our heavy equipment: chisels, sledgehammers, gads, crowbars, and safety equipment.

TEXAS ROCKHOUNDING DIVISIONS

For the purpose of this book, we divide Texas into five sections: East, Central, South, West, and the Panhandle. Below find the descriptions of the divisions.

- **East Texas:** East borders with Louisiana, north with Oklahoma, south with the Gulf, and west is I-35 from the north to Temple then continue on a straight line south through Bastrop to Corpus Christi
- **Central Texas:** East borders with East Texas from Oklahoma south to the junction of US 183 with US 77, then a line west to Devine and continue west to about 10 miles north of Quemado at the Rio Grande; west border of Central Texas continues north to Sweetwater then diagonally northeast to Wichita Falls
- **South Texas:** North borders with Central Texas, east with the southern border of East Texas and then the Gulf, and west is the Rio Grande
- **West Texas:** East part borders Central Texas, south is the Rio Grande, and north borders New Mexico; then from the Southwest corner of the Panhandle continue a straight line east to Sweetwater
- **Panhandle:** the rest

EAST TEXAS

After years of collecting in Texas, we thought of the eastern zone as being difficult—we have to admit that was a mistake. East Texas can be very prolific if one knows what they are doing.

A lot of the gathering here is of petrified wood. However, there actually is a great variety of other chalcedony as well as many varieties of fossils to pick up.

The prize among the wood is palm wood, which is the state rock. It is distinguished from other tree fossils by its monocotal tubes. Most trees have a vascular system that is composed of phloem and xylem pathways that ring the tree. The circulatory system of monocots is that of pairs of tubes bundled together. These are visible as small dots in a cross section. You may have to look closely as they can be very small.

Palm wood comes in a variety of colors that range from black, gray, or brown, or a mix of these. Some pieces will show strikes of red, yellow, orange, or blue. Almost all of this material is well siliconized and takes a great polish.

Like in the rest of Texas, rockhounding is primarily roadside in the east. The thick ground cover makes areas of erosion the best bet. However, a little scraping with a geological hammer or short handle rake will often reveal some treasures. Be a good rock hound and replace any divots you create. We do not want to be responsible for unnecessary erosion.

Gathering on private land is a possibility but obtaining permission can be challenging, time consuming, very fluid, and most likely will entail payment of a fee. The national forests might allow rockhounding with lots of restrictions. Check with the rangers before starting.

The weather in East Texas is more moderate than a lot of the rest of the state. It's hot in the summer and can be very humid. It rains a lot. The environment is very conducive to snake development. So be prepared.

1. Sabine River Woods

Land type: Forested road
GPS: Site A: 31.1730115 / -93.5636374, Site B: 31.1708611 / -93.5706109
Elevation: 170 feet
Best time of year: Winter, spring, fall
Land manager: The Sabine River Authority. This entity is a joint operation of both Louisiana and Texas. It is self-sustaining by selling electricity produced at the dam.
Material: Flint, jasper, petrified wood, agate
Tools: A geological hammer, spray bottle, and rake can be useful but are not required.
Vehicle type: 2-wheel is drive OK during dry periods for the first 0.8 mile. Otherwise 4-wheel drive is recommended.
Precautions and restrictions: There are some cables running through the area. Avoid those. The river banks are very slippery, and the river is fast. Be careful.
Accommodations: Camping at Toledo Bend State Park. There are also a few Forest Service campgrounds that might also be good collecting areas. There are a number of motels and hotels in Leesville, Louisiana.

Material buried in the river banks

Sites 1–3

Petrified wood imbedded in river banks

SPECIAL ATTRACTIONS

Excellent fishing in both the river and lake. Both waters hold good numbers and sizes of largemouth bass, blue catfish, crappie, and a number of other species. Visit the Leesville Art Park with displays of the works of local artists and the museum of West Louisiana. Learn about the history of the local area.

FINDING THE SITE

Toledo Bend Reservoir is located in Newton County. This area lies about 200 miles northeast of Houston, and it takes about three and half hours to get there. The Toledo Bend Reservoir is located at the eastern end of Texas. The dam is at the southern end of the lake. Though this site is in Texas, it is accessible through extreme western Louisiana. From Toledo Bend State Park go to junction LA 292 and LA 191 then continue south on LA 191 and cross into Texas where the road becomes TX 692. After 2.2 miles from the junction, turn left onto a rough road along the Sabine River. Drive to the bear sighting sign and park. This is Site A.

To get to Site B, return to TX 692 and after passing over the river, you will see a road off to the left. This is also worth checking out. Site B is located at the first right-hand turn after the bridge. Drive 0.2 mile to a parking area on the left.

Jasper collected at the Sabine River

The Sabine River Dam

ROCKHOUNDING

The river cuts through some prime petrified wood strata. However, the place has been known by collectors for a long time. It is quite picked over. Yet with due diligence, nice material is obtainable. You will notice small pieces of agate and flint. These are great for tumbling. There is no abundance here. We picked up a few handfuls including a very colorful mixed green, yellow, and red jasper in a half hour. There is a boat ramp that will take you down to the river, and you will be able to search farther along the bank.

At Site B, we found a number of pieces of flint and jasper by just wandering around.

2. Ayish Bayou Chalcedony

See map on page 3.
Land type: Forest on lake
GPS: 31.2658701 / -94.1107529
Elevation: 164 feet
Best time of year: Any time
Land manager: Texas Department of Transportation
Material: Chalcedony including agate, flint, jasper
Tools: A geological hammer, spray bottle, and short handle rake might be helpful but are not absolutely necessary.
Vehicle type: 2-wheel drive is fine.
Precautions and restrictions: There are some big ruts at the sides of the pavement. Do not get stuck.
Accommodations: There is a very lovely Corps of Engineers campground on Lake Sam Rayburn. It is called San Anton Campground and is a few miles from this site.

SPECIAL ATTRACTIONS

Great fishing in Lake Sam Rayburn. Largemouth bass are very numerous and large in this lake, which was formed by the damming of the Angelina River. They are caught year-round. Crappie and catfish are also numerous and result in an excellent year-round fishery. Bluegill and redear are present in prodigious numbers and great fun for the kids to catch. White bass are present but not in great numbers; however, they provide good fishing opportunities during the spring. This reservoir has a few special regulations. Familiarize yourself with them before fishing.

Visit the Patricia Huffman Smith NASA "Remembering Columbia" Museum, Hemphill; 409-787-4827; nasacolumbiamuseum.com. This museum is dedicated to the memory of Patricia Huffman Smith and the other astronauts of the Columbia spacecraft, which blew up upon reentry on its journey back to Earth from orbit on February 1, 2008, at 8:59 a.m.

The tour takes the individual on a trip passing through the spacecraft's first flight through its last. It also provides information on the recovery of Columbia and the crew of STS-107 and the process of the determination of the cause of the disaster. The museum has many items and artifacts on display from NASA and other agencies and the families of the crew of STS-107.

Ayish Bayou

The museum features a lot of great historical information about Shelby County, Texas. They have lots of interesting things to see and can answer a lot of questions you may have about the history.

FINDING THE SITE

Broaddus is a town in San Augustine County. It is about 150 miles from Houston and takes about two and a half hours to drive the distance. From the

Ayish Bayou flint

intersection of TX 147 and US 83 drive 10.3 miles east on US 83 to the boat ramp on the left (north). If you are coming from the east at the junction of US 83 and Texas Farm Road 1751 in Pineland, drive 7.3 miles west on US 83 to the public boat ramp on the right (north). Turn in and park out of the way. This ramp is used for access to Ayish Bayou, a popular fishing hole off Lake Sam Rayburn.

ROCKHOUNDING

This area's soil is created from sandy bands of Pleistocene origin. This was during the Ice Age and earlier Tertiary Period. Ayish Bayou is an inlet off the Angelina River in Texas. It begins about 7 miles north of San Augustine in northern San Augustine County, near the county line at Shelby, Texas. The Angelina River has been dammed, forming the Sam Rayburn Reservoir.

Search around the edges of the pavement of the boat ramp and also around the bank of the lake down below. There is easy access, and you can continue searching farther along the bank. You will notice pieces of nice flint and jasper at once. We picked up about ten chunks in 5 minutes.

3. Cassels-Boykin Park Jasper, Petrified Wood, and Agate

See map on page 3.
Land type: Forested lake and farm land
GPS: 31.2150161 / -94.3464386
Elevation: 162 feet
Best time of year: Any time of year
Land manager: Texas Department of Transportation
Material: Flint, jasper, agate, petrified wood
Tools: Rake, small pick
Vehicle type: Any vehicle
Precautions and restrictions: The lake can be very muddy and slippery. Walk carefully.
Accommodations: There is a very lovely Corps of Engineers campground on Lake Sam Rayburn. It is called San Anton Campground, which is a few miles from this site. There also are a number of private campgrounds and motels.

SPECIAL ATTRACTIONS

Great fishing in Lake Sam Rayburn. Largemouth bass are very numerous and large in this lake, which was formed by the damming of the Angelina River. They are caught year-round. Crappie and catfish are also numerous and result in an excellent year-round fishery. Bluegill and redear are present in prodigious numbers and great fun for the kids to catch. White bass are present but not in great numbers; however, they provide good fishing opportunities during the spring. This reservoir has a few special regulations. Familiarize yourself with them before fishing.

Visit the Patricia Huffman Smith NASA "Remembering Columbia" Museum, Hemphill; 409-787-4827; columbiamuseum@yahoo.com. This museum is dedicated to the memory of Patricia Huffman Smith and the other astronauts of the Columbia spacecraft, which blew up upon reentry on its journey back to Earth from orbit on February 1, 2008, at 8:59 a.m.

The tour takes the individual on a trip passing through the spacecraft's first flight through its last. It also provides information on the recovery of Columbia and the crew of STS-107 and the process of the determination of the cause of the disaster. The museum has many items and artifacts on display from NASA and other agencies and the families of the crew of STS-107.

This museum features a lot of great historical information about Shelby County, Texas! They have lots of interesting things and can answer a lot of questions you may have about the history. If you get a chance to go by, do. Be sure to check out the historical downtown square as well.

FINDING THE SITE
From the junction of US 83 and TX 147 drive over the Sam Rayburn Bridge. At 7.7 miles make a right onto Texas Farm Road 3123. Follow this 1 mile to a boat ramp at the end.

ROCKHOUNDING
Look for areas of erosion. You can also walk along the lake shore if the water is low enough. We picked up a handful of pretty tumblers in about 10 minutes. There also were a few larger pieces that would have made nice slicers but we left them for you.

Cassels-Boykin Park overview

Cassels-Boykin Park flint and jasper

4. Trinity Wood

Land type: Wooded flatland
GPS: 30.9538495 / -95.2983347
Elevation: 183 feet
Best time of year: Any time of year
Land manager: Texas Department of Transportation
Material: Petrified wood, jasper, flint
Tools: Geological hammer, rake, spray bottle
Vehicle type: Good road. Any type of vehicle is fine.
Precautions and restrictions: Park well off the road and turn on flashers. Watch for snakes during hot weather.
Accommodations: Lake Livingston State Park offers a fine camping opportunity. There are some lakeside campsites where one can fish from the bank. The state park sports some very pleasant hiking trails and a fishing pier. Make reservations early as this place is very busy. There are a number of inns and motels in Trinity as well as commercial RV resorts and campgrounds.

Trinity wood Texas Farm Road 3188 site

Sites 4–7

94

3188

4

356

5

Trinity

Lake L Dr

Pinecrest Rd

Lovelady

19

2712

4020

4030

6

Crockett

287

287

7

21

Trinity River

Midway

21

TX-OSR

45

75

7

Leona

75

Centerville

45

75

Madisonville

90

190

Normangee

TX-OSR

Marquez

7

79

7

79

Franklin

N

5 mi

5 km.

0

0

SPECIAL ATTRACTIONS

Trinity County Museum, located in Groveton, Texas, contains exhibits that promote education and research. Visitors can attend museum events, see exhibits, and access educational programs.

There is fishing in Lake Livingston. This lake was formed by the damming of the Trinity River. Besides all the usual lake species available, this body of water is known for its white bass fishery. These fish grow to prodigious sizes and are very plentiful here. There are a number of guide services available for hire as well as boat rental services.

FINDING THE SITE

This site is about 88 miles north of Houston, and it takes about an hour and a half to drive the distance. The GPS numbers are for the following point: From the junction of US 287 and TX 94, drive 12.9 miles south on TX 94 to Texas Farm Road 3188 and turn left. Go 2.3 miles on this road.

ROCKHOUNDING

There are lots of small pieces of petrified wood at this site. Some of it is float, but you'll get a lot more if you rake. You have a better chance of finding larger pieces if you dig a bit. Some of the petrified wood is palm wood. We gathered about a small plastic bag full in about 15 minutes. Do not limit yourself to our location. There is a lot of stuff all around the area. The biggest problem is finding a place to park. One might be better off doing some walking to the site than parking in a place that isn't safe.

Trinity wood flint and jasper

5. Lake L Drive Wood and Jasper

See map on page 12.
Land type: Forested and residential
GPS: 30.926385 / -95.3336117
Elevation: 205 feet
Best time of year: All year. it is hot in the summer and can be cold or snowing in winter.
Land manager: Texas Department of Transportation
Material: Petrified wood, jasper
Tools: Geological hammer, rake, spray bottle
Vehicle type: Good road. Any type of vehicle is fine.
Accommodations: Lake Livingston State Park offers a fine camping opportunity. There are some lakeside campsites where one can fish from the bank. The state park sports some very pleasant hiking trails and a fishing pier. Make reservations early as this place is very busy. There are a number of inns and motels in Trinity as well as commercial RV resorts and campgrounds.

Image of Lake L Drive

Lake L Drive material

SPECIAL ATTRACTIONS

Trinity County Museum, located in Groveton, contains exhibits that promote education and research. Visitors can attend museum events, see exhibits, and access educational programs.

There is fishing in Lake Livingston. This lake was formed by the damming of the Trinity River. Besides all the usual lake species available, this body of water is known for its white bass fishery. These fish grow to prodigious sizes and are very plentiful here. There are a number of guide services available for hire as well as boat rental services.

FINDING THE SITE

Trinity is about 100 miles north of Houston, and it takes about an hour and a half to drive there. From the junction of TX 94 and Texas Farm Road 3188 go 3.5 miles into Trinity. Turn left onto Emory Street and the next left onto Texas Farm Road 356 and travel 2.8 miles to Lake L Drive on the right. Turn onto Lake L Drive.

ROCKHOUNDING

The GPS numbers are for the corner of Lake L Drive and Texas Farm Road 356. We found petrified wood and jasper immediately. The site continues the entire length of Lake L Drive. Stop anywhere it is safe, and you will find material.

6. Crockett Petrified Wood and Palm Wood

See map on page 12.
Land type: Forested and farm land
GPS: 31.2239617 / -95.4687267
Elevation: 506 feet
Best time of year: All year but hot in the summer
Land manager: Texas Department of Transportation
Material: Petrified wood, palm wood, jasper, marine fossils
Tools: Geological hammer, spray bottle, rake
Vehicle type: Rough road but would be passable for 2-wheel drive in good weather
Precautions and restrictions: Road very narrow. Vehicles have to pull aside if another is met. There is no place to pull off, but there was little traffic when we were there enabling us to stop for a few minutes and look around. Use your flashers.

Accommodations: Davy Crockett National Forest offers camping. Besides the developed areas, individuals can take advantage of the dispersion camping throughout the national forest most of the time with the exception of hunting season. During winter, camping is restricted to certain areas for safety. Mission Tejas State Park, which is about 20 miles northeast of Crockett, offers camping. The sites have either all the amenities or they can be quite primitive.

Farm Road 4030

SPECIAL ATTRACTIONS
The Davy Crockett National Forest offers some good fishing opportunities

as well as a number of easy to difficult hiking trails. It is a fine place for wild-life observation and it is encouraged.

The Houston County Visitor Center and Museum offers displays ranging from cotton farming imple-ments to ox bows to railroad items. One of the feature exhibits is an old cotton gin. They offer teacher work-shops, tours, and lectures.

FINDING THE SITE

Crockett is a small city about 120 miles north of Houston, Texas. It takes less than 2 hours to drive the distance. To find the site, from the town of Crockett at the intersection of Texas Loop 304 and Texas Farm Road 2712, drive south 4.8 miles to the junction of Texas Farm Road 4030. Turn west (right) and travel 1.3 miles to the site. To leave you can continue straight ahead to the small town of Cut at the junction of TX 19.

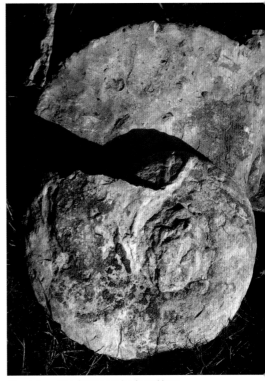

Very interesting fossils can be found here.

ROCKHOUNDING

On both sides of this small road, we found a variety of petrified wood, jasper, agate, and marine fossils. As we drove the road it appeared as though there was nothing there. Finally, after stopping the vehicle and getting out, the material became obvious. It was just that each piece had to be examined carefully. They are well worn. But after careful scrutiny, we noticed the value in them. Just about every piece was jasper and/or contained fossils. There is a lot of good collecting here.

7. Marquez Kosse Fossils

See map on page 12.
Land type: Forested but more open than sites to the east. It looks like land between forest and desert.
GPS: 31.2512313 / -96.3050518
Elevation: 407 feet
Best time of year: All year. It is hot in summer and can be cold in winter.
Land manager: Texas Department of Transportation
Material: Marine fossils, bivalves, gastropods
Tools: Geological hammer, garden shovel, short rake, spray bottle
Vehicle type: Good highway. Any vehicle will be OK.
Precautions and restrictions: Park well off the road. Texans drive very fast. Use your flashers.
Accommodations: The small Fort Parker State Park provides camping. The park offers RV sites and tent sites with water and electricity. For those who don't need an electric outlet at their site, they provide water-only sites. There also are a number of commercial campgrounds, RV parks, and resorts nearby. Motels and other accommodations are also within close driving distance.

The site from the road

SPECIAL ATTRACTIONS

Fort Parker State Park sports a nice fishing pier on a 750-acre lake that contains largemouth bass, both white and black crappie, and medium to large blue catfish. Fishing is fair at the lake in the state park.

The park maintains 7 miles of hiking and biking trails. Wildlife observation is a favorite activity and lots of fun. There is a great diversity and abundance of species as the park straddles two different ecosystems.

Well-defined fossils here

FINDING THE SITE

Marquez is a town located about 70 miles southeast of Waco in Leon County. It takes about 1 hour and 15 minutes to drive there from the city. From the junction of TX 7 and US 79 in downtown Marquez, travel 2.9 miles heading west on TX 7. You are now at the GPS numbers.

Well-defined fossils here

ROCKHOUNDING

The fossils here include but are not limited to bivalve and gastropods. Petrified wood is also rather abundant but is not polishable due to lack of silica content. These were deposited during the Paleocene Epoch. This area is close to a division between the Upper Cretaceous and Lower Tertiary formations. The soils are sandy, and there is rather light forestation. This provides the perfect environment for erosion and thus the exposure of the fossils. As of this writing, there were piles of red limestone at the side of the road. The fossils were very abundant. Do not limit yourselves to this exact location. There are many other areas nearby that contain the same material. In fact, these fossils can be found almost all the way to Kosse.

8. Lake Somerville Jasper, Flint, and Petrified Wood

Land type: Pine forest and farm
GPS: 30.3358064 / -96.5425644
Elevation: 238 feet
Best time of year: All year. It can be cold in the winter and hot in the summer.
Land manager: City of Somerville
Material: Jasper, petrified wood, agate, tektites
Tools: Geological hammer, garden shovel, short hand rake, spray bottle
Vehicle type: Good highway. Any vehicle would be OK.
Precautions and restrictions: Park well off the road. Use your flashers.
Accommodations: The park provides camping. On the lake you will also find Lake Somerville State Park. This park offers primitive camping as well as full hookup RV sites and everything in-between. Motels can be found in and around Somerville.

Somerville Lake from the park

Sites 8–12

SPECIAL ATTRACTIONS

The manager's large fossil collection could be of interest to most rock hounds.

Fishing in Lake Somerville is excellent. White bass anglers know this lake well as a high-quality fishery, especially during the spring spawning run. However, the lake offers very good fishing for hybrid striped bass, channel catfish, and crappie as well. Largemouth bass fishing is very good with catches of fish up to 10 pounds plus.

There are many miles of hiking and equestrian trails in this park, and wildlife observation is a popular activity.

The Somerville Historical Museum offers insight into the past of this area of Texas. The railway connection becomes immediately evident as the visitor is welcomed by an illustrated miniature wooden locomotive. Tours are offered as well as workshops upon occasion.

FINDING THE SITE

Somerville is a city in Burleson County. It is about 95 miles east of Austin and about 90 miles northwest of Houston. It takes about an hour and a half to drive there from either city. From the town of Somerville, turn west from TX 36 onto Thornberry Drive. Go 1.5 miles to the dam, turn right, and proceed

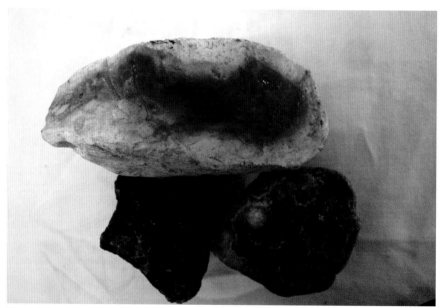

Material from Somerville Lake

to the entrance of Welch Park, which is on the lake. The park has an entrance fee.

ROCKHOUNDING

Collecting is allowed along the lake on the grounds in the park. Jasper is quite common, and petrified wood is also found. We found lots of small pieces of petrified wood, jasper, and flint. It was rather easy collecting. Do not limit yourself to this exact location. There is a lot of material in the area.

While the area is known for tektites, they are extremely rare. Tektites come in many different colors. These can be but are not limited to black, green, brown, gray, or a mixture of all colors. They are a natural glass formed from terrestrial debris when a meteorite impacts the Earth. The heat of the impact melts the surrounding soils. The term was first used by Austrian geologist Franz Eduard Suess. They are gravel size and generally range from about 0.1 inch to 15 inches in size. We did not find any, but that doesn't mean that you won't hit the jackpot with diligent searching.

9. Ledbetter Jasper and Petrified Wood

See map on page 21.
Land type: Forested and farmland
GPS: 30.1193194 / -96.7921532
Elevation: 350 feet
Best time of year: Any time there is no snow on the ground
Land manager: Texas Department of Transportation
Material: Jasper, petrified wood
Tools: Geological hammer, short handle rake, garden shovel, spray bottle
Vehicle type: Good highway. Any vehicle type is fine.
Precautions and restrictions: Be sure to pull completely off the pavement; if this isn't possible, drive to a place where it is. Carefully open your vehicle door, making sure there is no one speeding down the road at you. Use your warning flashers.
Accommodations: Lake Somerville State Park is about 30 miles north of Ledbetter and takes about 35 minutes to drive there. This park offers primitive camping as

Ledbetter site from your car window

well as full hookup RV sites and everything in-between. There are many miles of hiking and equestrian trails. There also are a number of private campgrounds and RV parks and resorts nearby. Motels can be found throughout the area.

SPECIAL ATTRACTIONS

Fishing in Lake Somerville is excellent. White bass anglers know this lake well as a high-quality fishery, especially during the spring spawning run. However, the lake offers very good fishing for hybrid striped bass, channel catfish, and crappie as well. Largemouth bass fishing is very good with catches of fish up to 10 pounds plus. The state park offers loaner fishing rods, and boats and kayaks are available to rent.

The Somerville Historical Museum offers insight into the past of this area of Texas. The railway connection becomes immediately evident as the visitor is welcomed by an illustrated miniature wooden locomotive. Tours are offered as well as workshops upon occasion.

FINDING THE SITE

Ledbetter is an unincorporated town in far northern Fayette County. It is about 65 miles east of Austin and takes about 1 hour and 15 minutes to drive there from the big city.

In the town of Ledbetter at the junction of US 290 and Texas Farm Road 1291, head south on Texas Farm Road 1291 for 2.9 miles. That's the location of the GPS numbers.

ROCKHOUNDING

After driving along and not finding any areas of erosion, we decided to stop and scrape through the grass. To our surprise, every stone that was exposed was either jasper, petrified wood, or agate. Most of what we found was tumbler size, but we also dug up a few slicers. After a few more stops, we decided that the location is very prolific and stopping anywhere would produce fine material.

Common find at the Ledbetter site

10. Waldeck and Roundtop Chalcedony

See map on page 21.
Land type: Pine forest and farmland
GPS: 30.0572794 / -96.8021724
Elevation: 440 feet
Best time of year: Spring, winter (when there is no snow on ground), and autumn. It gets very hot and humid in the summer.
Land manager: Texas Department of Transportation
Material: Chalcedony of every description including but not limited to jasper, flint, agate, petrified wood
Tools: Geological hammer, short handle rake, spray bottle
Vehicle type: Good roads all the way. Any vehicle is fine.
Precautions and restrictions: Park well off the road. Some of the shoulders are quite narrow in this area. If you cannot pull off the pavement at a particular

Looking across the road from the Waldeck and Roundtop site.

location, drive a bit farther to a place where you can. Always use your flashers when leaving your vehicle on the side of the road. Beware of snakes during warm weather. They do well in this type of environment.

Accommodations: Buescher State Park in Smithville offers full hookup or partial hookup camping. Every effort has been made to leave this park as natural as possible. It is about 33 miles northwest of Waldeck and takes about a half hour to drive there from Waldeck.

Lake Somerville State Park is about 30 miles north of Ledbetter and takes about 35 minutes to drive there. This park offers primitive camping as well as full hookup RV sites and everything in-between. There are many miles of hiking and equestrian trails.

There also are a number of private campgrounds and RV parks and resorts nearby. Motels can be found throughout the area.

SPECIAL ATTRACTIONS

Buescher State Park offers a number of hiking and biking trails. The Winding Woodlands Trail is 6 miles long and passes through a corridor of towering

Waldeck jasper and agate

loblolly pine trees. It is extremely scenic and provides good insight into the what the natural environment of this area looks like.

Buescher State Park sports a small lake that is stocked with fish periodically. They also have fishing rod loaners and boats and canoes for rent.

Fishing in Lake Somerville at the Lake Somerville State Park is excellent. White bass anglers know this lake well as a high-quality fishery, especially during the spring spawning run. However, the lake offers very good fishing for hybrid striped bass, channel catfish, and crappie as well. Largemouth bass fishing is very good with catches of fish up to 10 pounds plus. The state park offers loaner fishing rods, and boats and kayaks are available to rent.

FINDING THE SITE

Waldeck is an unincorporated town in northern Fayette County. It is about 70 miles east of Austin, and it takes about 1 hour and 15 minutes to drive there from the state capital. This site is at the corner of Texas Farm Road 1291 and Texas Farm Road 2145. There is a pullout on the northeast corner of the intersection. There is a farm directly across from the site on the west side of the road and a church on the south side of Texas Farm Road 2145.

ROCKHOUNDING

This location was one of those serendipitous finds that doesn't occur very often in the rockhounding business. After driving from the Ledbetter site, we noticed a small parking area. There were a couple of piles of fill in it. Soon after looking at the dumping, it became obvious that they were composed of hundreds if not thousands of good-size chunks of chalcedony. The variety was incredible. We left them intact for others to enjoy. We're not sure whether that particular pile will be there when you are in the area. However, keep your eyes open for others. Roadwork is a continual process.

11. La Grange Petrified Wood and Jasper

See map on page 21.
Land type: Pine forest and farms
GPS: 30.0327233 / -96.885295
Elevation: 266 feet
Best time of year: All year. It is very hot in the summer and can be cold in winter, possibly with snow. covered.
Land manager: Texas Department of Transportation
Material: Petrified wood, jasper
Tools: Geological hammer, short handle rake, garden shovel, spray bottle
Vehicle type: Good roads. 2-wheel drive is sufficient.
Precautions and restrictions: Park well off the pavement. If you cannot, drive a little farther and walk back. Use your warning flashers.

View of the site

Accommodations: Buescher State Park in Smithville is about 20 miles northwest of La Grange. This park offers full hookup or partial hookup camping. Every effort has been made to leave this park as natural as possible. There are a number of commercial RV parks and campgrounds near La Grange. Motels are available nearby.

SPECIAL ATTRACTIONS

Kreische State Historic Site: Heinrich Ludwig Kreische was a master stone smith. He was a German immigrant, and in 1849 he purchased 172 acres of land including the Dawson/Mier tomb, now known as Monument Hill. Kreische built a three-story house and he and his family used it as their home. During the 1860s, he started one of the first commercial breweries in Texas. His beer was considered excellent because it was made with local spring water from his property.

This property has now been set up as a museum. The visitor can pass through the ruins of this once bustling brewery and envision how this area's citizens would come and enjoy a pint of Kreische's Bluff Beer while looking out toward the beautiful Texas landscape. The Kreische Brewery and home are listed in the National Register of Historic Places.

Typical material found at La Grange

Biking and hiking in Buescher State Park Fishing are also popular activities in this park. The lake is stocked on a regular basis. Canoes and boats can be rented for a day on the water.

FINDING THE SITE

La Grange is a small city in Fayette County about 60 miles southeast of Austin. It takes about 1 hour and 10 minutes to drive there from the big city. At the junction of US 77 and Texas Farm Road 2145, travel 6.1 miles north on US 77 to Bear Creek Road, aka Texas CR 145. Turn east and drive 1 mile to Texas CR 152, aka Owl Creek Road. The GPS numbers were taken at 0.2 mile before the bridge.

ROCKHOUNDING

This area is not as prolific as others, but enough can be found to make the stop worthwhile. Do not limit yourself to the GPS numbers we provide. It was a good spot to pull off the road. We noticed material quite quickly. There is material all along Owl Creek Road. Petrified palm wood is in the mix but not in any abundance.

12. Smithville Petrified Wood and Jasper

See map on page 21.

Land type: Farmland, ranches, and sparsely forested

GPS: 30.4359161 / -97.1631515

Elevation: 325 feet

Best time of year: Spring and autumn. This site can be accessed in the winter if there is no snow on the ground, and it can be very hot in the summer.

Land manager: Texas Department of Transportation

Material: Petrified wood, flint, jasper

Tools: Geological hammer, short handle rake, garden shovel, spray bottle

Vehicle type: Good highway. 2-wheel drive is sufficient.

Precautions and restrictions: Park well off the pavement. If you cannot, drive a little farther and walk back. Use your warning flashers.

Accommodations: Buescher State Park is located just north of Smithville, Texas. The park consists of 1,016.7 acres of public land. This park offers a variety of

Rockhound paradise

campsites including ones with water and electricity. The electric hookup can be either 20- or 30-amp. At a reduced rate they have sites with water only and primitive camping, which is camping with no amenities available. These are walk-in sites. Besides the state park, there are a number of private campgrounds and RV resorts in the area. Motels are available in Smithville and other nearby locations.

Nice material at Smithville

SPECIAL ATTRACTIONS

Biking and hiking in Buescher State Park. Fishing is also a popular activity in this park. The lake is stocked on a regular basis. Canoes and boats can be rented for a day on the water.

It is absolutely necessary that if you visit Smithville an image of the largest gingerbread man must be taken before you leave. His name is Smitty, and he is located next to the railroad depot. He was created in 2009 and made Guinness World Records. The town used the original baking sheet to create and erect a statue of the ol' boy.

A visit to the James H. Long Railroad Park and Museum is certainly worth your time. They allow folks to climb up into the historic rail train cars to get a good look around.

Smithville sports a charming downtown area. A walk around the village is well worth one's time.

FINDING THE SITE

Smithville is a small city in Bastrop County about 40 miles southeast of Austin. It's about 45 minutes to drive there from the big city. This site is located north of the town of Smithville. From the junction of TX 71, Texas Loop 230, and Texas Farm Road 153 turn north on Texas Farm Road 153. After the turn, we found several very large mounds of fill. This is where the GPS was taken.

ROCKHOUNDING

We immediately found petrified wood, flint, and jasper in moderate quantities. This material can be found for at least a half mile north on Texas Farm Road 153. Petrified palm wood is in the mix but only in small quantities.

13. North Sulphur River Ladonia Fossil Park

Land type: Piney woods, thick pine stands and oak hickory, magnolia, gum, and hardwood forests
GPS: 33.4540053 / -95.9600592
Elevation: 627 feet
Best time of year: All year except when there is snow on the ground. It can be very hot in summer.
Land manager: Upper Trinity Regional Water District
Material: Fossils
Tools: Geological hammer, short handle rake, garden shovel, spray bottle
Vehicle type: Good road all the way to the site. 2-wheel drive sufficient.
Precautions and restrictions: The access to the river is rather steep. Be prepared for the descent. Wear good boots as there is some broken glass in the river and on the bank. it can be very hot in the summer, bring a lot of water.

A good water level for fossil hunting
Mitchell

Site 13

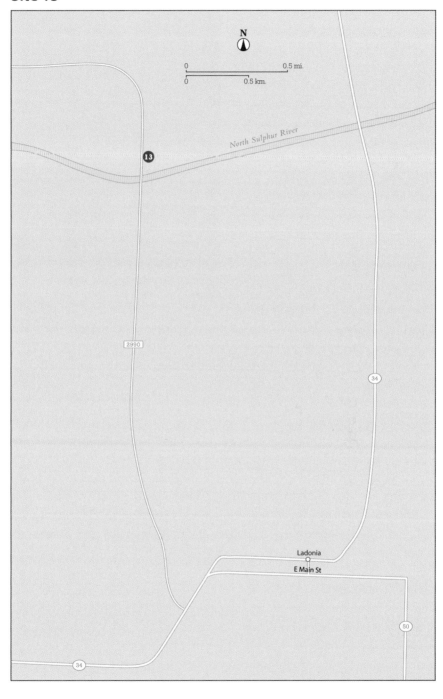

Accommodations: Cooper Lake State Park is about 33 miles southeast of Ladonia. It takes about 40 minutes to drive there. The park offers a variety of camping experiences including full hookup sites. Besides the park, there are a number of commercial RV resorts and campgrounds. Hotels and motels can be found nearby.

A typical variety of fossils from Ladonia *Mitchell*

SPECIAL ATTRACTIONS

Ladonia Fossil Day is put on once a year. The city hosts a meet and greet for all those interested in fossil collecting. Experienced fossil hunters will be available to ID your finds or answer any questions you have. Hot dogs will be served by the fire department. Bring your own chairs. Books will be available, and the park's T-shirts and cups will be for sale.

Cooper Lake State Park offers all the usual activities: fishing, hiking, biking, paddling, etc.

FINDING THE SITE

Ladonia is a town in Fannin County. It is about 80 miles northeast of Dallas with a drive time of about 1 hour and 25 minutes. From the junction of TX 34 and Texas Farm Road 2990 head north on Texas Farm Road 2990 for 2.1 miles. After crossing the river, you will see the signs for the park and parking lot.

Keep in mind that this is only a temporary location as the access area is being relocated. Check with the Upper Trinity Regional Water District for updates.

ROCKHOUNDING

The North Sulphur River has been a famous fossil collecting area for a long time. But it never seems to become depleted because after each rain more treasures are exposed. This is a partial list of what might be found: mosasaur bone, plesiosaur bone, sharkstooth, ammonite, and arrowheads.

CENTRAL TEXAS

This section of Texas, as with most areas, has a great number of rockhounding possibilities. The primary materials here are agate, petrified wood, jasper, and flint. These are often quite colorful and make excellent jewelry or display pieces when polished.

Some of the agate is clear with myriad colors in swirls. The wood includes some small pieces of palm wood. These are often very colorful and well agatized, appropriate for cutting.

Roadside collecting here is excellent and very widespread. The area around Choke Canyon Reservoir used to be a favorite collecting site for rock hounds. However, it is now a state park and off limits. But there is no need to despair because the roadside in proximity of the lake can be littered with material available for pick up.

The region around Zapata and Falcon Reservoir is much the same. As of this writing, it is OK to collect along the shoreline as long as one avoids Falcon Lake State Park. Again, many of the roadsides are covered with fine material.

Weather-wise, collecting is good all year. It can be extremely hot in the summer. So make sure you carry a lot of water and sunscreen. We enjoy the area in the winter as the temperatures are usually quite pleasant.

Extra caution should be taken during warm weather here as well as all throughout Texas. This area holds a particularly large population of reptiles. Always carry a snake stick and rattle, and brush with it before stepping close. There may be a very upset critter under your foot if you don't. Look a stone completely over before putting it in the bag. You do not want any unwelcome hitchhikers.

14. Hubbard Creek Reservoir Hematite

Land type: Rolling hills with oak trees, woodland, and grass hills
GPS: 32.8212451 / -98.9540026
Elevation: 1,250 feet
Best time of year: Spring, summer, fall
Land manager: Texas Department of Transportation
Material: Hematite
Tools: Geological hammer, short handle rake, garden shovel, spray bottle
Vehicle type: Though the last mile of the road is gravel, it appears to be well maintained. 2-wheel drive is sufficient.
Precautions and restrictions: Very difficult finding a place to pull off at the location. Drive ahead up the slope to where it levels off and pulling off is possible. Walk back.
Accommodations: Copper Breaks State Park is about 86 miles northwest of Throckmorton with a drive time of about 1 hour and 15 minutes. They offer a

Start looking where the road elevation increases

Sites 14–21

Look for reddish stones

variety of camping experiences. The park does not have full hookup sites but they do offer parking with electricity and water. Besides the state park, there are a number of commercial RV parks and resorts in the area. Motels are located in the Quanah area.

SPECIAL ATTRACTIONS

Copper Breaks State Park landscape is very scenic with mesquite- and grass-covered hills. It is a great place to do some bird watching for a number of species of ducks, roadrunners, meadowlarks, quail, doves, great blue herons, cardinals, flickers, bluebirds, kites, hawks, mockingbirds, a few species of owls, and many others.

Mammals also abound. On an early morning or late evening walk, you may spot mule deer, rabbits, raccoons, armadillos, opossums, bobcats, porcupines, and coyotes. A few species of frogs, toads, turtles, and lizards also call the park home.

Hiking is also a popular activity at the park. The trails can be used for walking or biking. The lake is stocked with rainbow trout and catfish. Loaner tackle is available.

FINDING THE SITE

Throckmorton is about 130 miles northwest of Fort Worth. It takes about 2 hours and 15 minutes to drive the distance. From south of the town of Throckmorton at the junction of US 283 and US 183, drive southeast on US 183 for 22.8 miles to the junction of Texas Farm Road 274. Turn west on Texas Farm Road 274 and drive 0.9 mile. Turn south on Texas Farm Road 278 and proceed 1 mile. Turn east on Water District Road 277 and drive behind the dam 1.2 miles to the site. Immediately before the location, the road follows a track below the dam. The site is located where the road proceeds up an incline at the end of the dam.

If you are coming from Breckenridge at the junction of US 180 and US 183, drive north 7.7 miles to the junction of Texas Farm Road 274. Then follow the above directions.

ROCKHOUNDING

We searched the area for about a half hour and found only one piece of suspected hematite because of its rust-colored streak. It was confirmed to be iron ore upon our return to our workshop. After grinding the suspected piece on a wheel, the metallic color was revealed. We do not feel there is much material at this location, but perhaps you will have better luck than us in locating some.

15. Cisco Marine Fossils

See map on page 39.

Land type: Cross timbers and grand prairie; post and live oak; woodland and grass prairies

GPS: 32.4869867 / -99.0020367

Elevation: 1,691 feet

Best time of year: Spring, summer, fall

Land manager: Texas Department of Transportation

Material: Marine fossils

Tools: Geological hammer, short handle rake, garden shovel, spray bottle

Vehicle type: Good highway all the way to the site. 2-wheel drive sufficient.

Precautions and restrictions: Be sure to pull completely off the pavement. Use your warning flashers.

Accommodations: Lake Brownwood State Park is about 47 miles south of Cisco. It takes about 49 minutes to drive the distance. This park offers a variety of camping opportunities including full hookup sites and primitive camping. The park also sports a historic cabin to rent out to campers. There also are a number of private campgrounds and RV parks as well as motels in the area.

Cisco fossil site

Typical fossils found at Cisco

SPECIAL ATTRACTIONS

Fishing for largemouth bass up to 12 pounds in Lake Brownwood is good, and crappie fishing is excellent. In addition, the lake offers excellent white bass fishing especially in the spring. Flathead and blue catfish grow to good sizes here as do the channel catfish. The kids can enjoy fishing for sunfish. The park offers loaner tackle to the public.

Besides fishing there are other water sports available. These include paddling and water skiing as well as jet skiing.

The park boasts 6 miles of hiking trails and also has a biking trail.

FINDING THE SITE

Cisco is a city in Eastland County. It is about 105 miles southwest of Fort Worth, and it takes about an hour and a half to drive the distance. From the town of Cisco at the junction of TX 6 and US 183, which is east 6th Street, turn north on TX 6 and drive for 10 miles.

ROCKHOUNDING

This was another serendipitous find, a random stop along the road. We found very interesting worm impressions, along with some crinoid stems and a few with heads.

16. Mineral Wells Fossil Park

See map on page 39.
Land type: Cross timbers and grand prairie; post and live oak; woodland and grass prairies
GPS: 32.8260439 / -98.1904583
Elevation: 773 feet
Best time of year: All year as long as no snow is on the ground. It can be very hot in summer.
Land manager: Mineral Wells Parks and Recreation Department
Material: Pennsylvanian Era fossils
Tools: Small zip bags for keeping your finds organized, knee pads for crawling around, small garden shovel
Vehicle type: Good road all the way to the site. 2-wheel drive is sufficient.
Precautions and restrictions: Enter and exit the collecting area at designated points only. Area has dangerous drop- offs, steep slopes, and loose soil. Encounters with dangerous insects/animals are possible. Folks are urged to visit in the early morning and late evening during the summer. Bring lots of water if you expect to spend some time here.

Entrance to mineral wells fossil site

The trail heading into the fossil pit

Accommodations: Lake Mineral Wells State Park is about 5 miles east of Mineral Wells and it takes about 10 minutes to drive there. This park offers a variety of camping opportunities including sites with 50- or 30-amp electricity and water-only sites.

SPECIAL ATTRACTIONS

Fishing at the lake is rated good to excellent. Six fishing piers are located around the shoreline. Besides fishing, the park offers a number of hiking and biking trails. Some come to this park to do rock climbing.

There are a number of mineral bathhouses in and around Mineral Wells. It sure would feel good relaxing in a warm bath after a day of rigorous rockhounding.

FINDING THE SITE

This site is located a few miles northwest of the city of Mineral Wells. Follow these directions carefully. From Mineral Wells at the junction of US 281 and US 180, drive west on US 180 for 2.4 miles to a junction with Indian Creek Road. At this fork, bear right onto Indian Creek Road. Follow the Indian Creek Road signs carefully, as the road appears to go straight but it doesn't. That is another road. You will be turning right at a number of corners. Also,

Typical fossils found at mineral wells

make note of the small signs that direct you to the park. Drive 2.5 miles on Indian Creek Road to its end at the fossil park.

ROCKHOUNDING

This is a wonderful spot for both the seasoned and amateur fossil collector. It was set up by the Dallas Paleontology Society and is maintained by the City of Mineral Wells. Folks have the opportunity to collect excellent well-preserved "Pennsylvanian Period" fossils with ease and abundance. These fossils have been dated to be just over 300 million years old. The finds include but are not limited to crinoids (sea lilies), echinoids (urchins), brachiopods, pelecypods (clams and oysters), bryozoans, corals, trilobites (arthropods), plants, and even primitive sharks. You are free to keep what you find but for personal use only. No commercial digging is allowed.

17. Cool Marine Fossils

See map on page 39.

Land type: Cross timbers and grand prairie; post and live oak; woodland and grass prairies
GPS: 32.7961067 / -97.9758217
Elevation: 1,089 feet
Best time of year: Spring, summer, fall
Land manager: Texas Department of Transportation
Material: Marine fossils
Tools: Geological hammer, short handle rake, garden shovel, spray bottle
Vehicle type: Good highway to the site. 2-wheel drive is sufficient.
Precautions and restrictions: Be sure to pull completely off the pavement. Use your warning flashers.
Accommodations: Lake Mineral Wells State Park is about 5 miles east of Mineral Wells, and it takes about 10 minutes to drive there. This park offers a variety of camping opportunities including sites with 50- or 30-amp electricity and water-only sites. There also are a number of private RV campgrounds and resorts in the area. Motels and hotels abound nearby.

Road view of site

Typical fossils found at Cool

SPECIAL ATTRACTIONS

Fishing at the lake is rated good to excellent. Six fishing piers are located around the shoreline. Besides fishing, the park offers a number of hiking and biking trails. Some folks come to this park to do rock climbing.

There are a number of mineral bathhouses in and around Mineral Wells. It sure would feel good relaxing in a warm bath after a day of rigorous rockhounding.

FINDING THE SITE

Cool is a town in Parker County. It is about 45 miles west of Fort Worth with a drive time of under an hour. From Mineral Wells at the junction of US 281 and US 180, drive east on US 180 for 8.4 miles to an exposed road cut. This is just past the town of Cool.

ROCKHOUNDING

The Upper and Lower Cretaceous eras are exposed in this area as well as the Pennsylvanian. The marine fossils from those eras are abundant along with some nice jasper, flint, agate, and petrified wood. Do not limit yourselves to this site. The material can be found almost anywhere you stop along the road.

18. Carter Road 51 Marine Fossils

See map on page 39.

Land type: Cross timbers and grand prairie; post and live oak; woodland and grass prairies; rolling hills and housing developments

GPS: 32.9049443 / -97.7236075

Elevation: 1,191 feet

Best time of year: All year as long as no snow is on the ground. It can be very hot in summer.

Land manager: Texas Department of Transportation

Material: Marine fossils

Tools: Geological hammer, short handle rake, garden shovel, spray bottle

Vehicle type: Good road all the way to the site. 2-wheel drive is sufficient.

Precautions and restrictions: Be sure to pull completely off the pavement. Use your warning flashers. This road can be very busy.

Accommodations: Lake Mineral Wells State Park is about 5 miles east of Mineral Wells, and it takes about 10 minutes to drive there. This park offers a variety of camping opportunities including sites with 50- or 30-amp electricity and water-only sites. There also are a number of private RV campgrounds and resorts in the area. Motels and hotels abound nearby.

Road view of site

Typical bivalve fossil from Route 51

SPECIAL ATTRACTIONS

Fishing at the lake is rated good to excellent. Six fishing piers are located around the shoreline. Besides fishing, the park offers a number of hiking and biking trails. Some folks come to this park to do rock climbing.

There are a number of mineral bathhouses in and around Mineral Wells. It sure would feel good relaxing in a warm bath after a day of rigorous rockhounding.

FINDING THE SITE

Carter is an unincorporated area and census-designated place in Parker County. It is about 33 miles northwest of Fort Worth with a drive time of about 50 minutes. From the town of Weatherford at the junction of US 180 and Texas Farm Road 51, drive north on Texas Farm Road 51 for 11.4 miles. You will be in a road cut with a new development behind it.

ROCKHOUNDING

Pennsylvanian fossils will be apparent as soon as you step out of your vehicle. Some of these are of a substantial size. The site we give was right outside the fence of a residential home and we were barked at the entire time. Do not limit yourselves to this location. Fossils can be found almost anywhere within a few miles of the given location.

19. Weatherford Marine Fossils

See map on page 39.
Land type: Cross timbers and grand prairie; post and live oak; woodland and grass prairies; rRolling hills
GPS: 32.6256968 / -97.7764906
Elevation: 434 feet
Best time of year: All year as long as no snow is on the ground. It can be very hot in summer.
Land manager: Texas Department of Transportation
Material: Marine fossils
Tools: Geological hammer, short handle rake, garden shovel, spray bottle
Vehicle type: Good road all the way to the site. 2-wheel drive is sufficient.
Precautions and restrictions: Be sure to pull completely off the pavement. Use your warning flashers. This road can be very busy.
Accommodations: Lake Mineral Wells State Park is about 26 miles southwest of Carter and it takes about a half hour to drive there. This park offers a variety of camping opportunities. They offer sites with 50- and 30-amp electricity service as well as some with water only. There are a number of private RV parks and campgrounds in the area as well as motels and motor lodges.

View from the road

Typical fossils from Weatherford

SPECIAL ATTRACTIONS

Fishing at the lake is rated good to excellent. Six fishing piers are located around the shoreline. Besides fishing, the park offers a number of hiking and biking trails. Some come to this park to do rock climbing.

There are a number of mineral bathhouses in and around Mineral Wells. It sure would feel good relaxing in a warm bath after a day of rigorous rockhounding.

FINDING THE SITE

Weatherford is a suburb of Fort Worth in Parker County. It is 29 miles from the big city, and the drive takes about 35 minutes. From the junction of Texas Farm Road 51/TX 171 and US 180 in Weatherford, drive south on Texas Farm Road 51/TX 171 for 4.3 miles to where the roads separate. Bear right onto Texas Farm Road 51 and travel 5.4 miles.

ROCKHOUNDING

Pennsylvanian Era fossils are quite abundant, and you will see them as soon as you step out of your vehicle. Some of these are very well preserved. Do not limit yourselves to this location. Fossils can be found almost anywhere within a few miles of the given location.

20. Hood County Fossils

Road view of site

See map on page 39.
Land type: Cross timbers and grand prairie; post and live oak; woodland and grass prairies; rolling hills and residential
GPS: 32.526816 / -97.799381
Elevation: 799 feet
Best time of year: All year as long as no snow is on the ground. It can be very hot in summer.
Land manager: Texas Department of Transportation
Material: Marine fossils
Tools: Geological hammer, short handle rake, garden shovel, spray bottle
Vehicle type: Good road all the way to the site. 2-wheel drive is sufficient.
Precautions and restrictions: Be sure to pull completely off the pavement. Use your warning flashers. This road is narrow in places and busy, and pulling off the pavement can be difficult.
Accommodations: Lake Mineral Wells State Park is about 30 miles northwest of this site, and it takes about 36 minutes to drive the distance. This park offers a variety of camping opportunities including water and electric sites as well as primitive camping.

Typical fossils found at Hood County

SPECIAL ATTRACTIONS

Fishing at the lake is rated good to excellent. Six fishing piers are located around the shoreline. Besides fishing, the park offers a number of hiking and biking trails. Some come to this park to do rock climbing.

There are a number of mineral bathhouses in and around Mineral Wells. It sure would feel good relaxing in a warm bath after a day of rigorous rockhounding.

FINDING THE SITE

Weatherford is a suburb of Fort Worth in Parker County. It is 29 miles from the big city, and the drive takes about 35 minutes. From the junction of Texas Farm Road 51/TX 171 and US 180 in Weatherford, drive south on Texas Farm Road 51/TX 171 for 4.3 miles until the roads separate. Bear right onto Texas Farm Road 51 and travel 13.4 miles.

ROCKHOUNDING

You have to dig to find fossils here. It also takes careful examination to discern the ancient organisms. Oysters and brachiopods are quite abundant at this location. Please fill in your holes after digging.

21. Granbury Marine Fossils

See map on page 39.

Land type: Cross timbers and grand prairie; post and live oak; woodland and grass prairies; rolling hills and residential

GPS: 32.3574581 / -97.7723876

Elevation: 1,040 feet

Best time of year: All year as long as no snow is on the ground. It can be very hot in summer.

Land manager: Texas Department of Transportation

Material: Marine fossils

Tools: Geological hammer, short handle rake, garden shovel, spray bottle

Vehicle type: Good road all the way to the site. 2-wheel drive is sufficient.

Precautions and restrictions: Be sure to pull completely off the pavement. Use your warning flashers. This road is narrow in places and busy, and pulling off the pavement can be difficult.

Accommodations: Cleburne State Park is about 30 miles southeast of Granbury. It takes about 35 minutes to drive the distance. The park offers a variety of camping experiences from full hookup to primitive camping. Besides the state park, there are a number of private RV parks and resorts. Hotels and motels are located nearby.

Image of site

SPECIAL ATTRACTIONS

Cleburne State Park is a fun place for the entire family. Hiking, biking, nature viewing, fishing, paddling, and many other activities are part of the experience.

Dinosaur Valley State Park is nearby. Here you can be taken back millions of years and see where the dinosaurs roamed. Do-it-yourself tours as well as guided tours are available.

FINDING THE SITE

Granbury is a city in and the county seat of Hood County. It is 38 miles southwest of Fort Worth with a drive time of about 50 minutes. From the town of Granbury at the junction of Texas Farm Road 51 and US 377, turn west on US 377, drive 7 blocks, and at the traffic light turn south onto South Morgan Street, which is also TX 144. Drive 6.1 miles to the site.

ROCKHOUNDING

There are a lot of marine fossils at this site. It looks like they are mostly Pennsylvanian, mainly consisting of brachiopods, bivalves, and gastropods. There is some float here, but a bit of scraping with a rake or geological hammer may reveal some that are hidden underground. Do not limit yourselves to this one site; fossils can be found for a number of miles around this location.

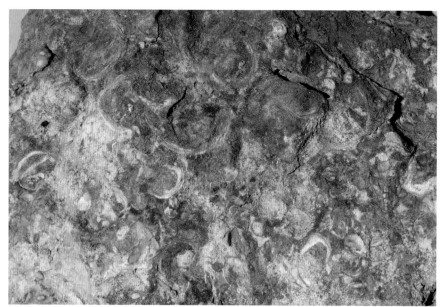
Material at site

22. Meridian Fossils

Land type: Lightly forested, ranches and farms
GPS: 31.9265267 / -97.6166938
Elevation: 673 feet
Best time of year: Fall, spring, and winter if snow is not present
Land manager: Texas Department of Transportation
Material: Fossils including bivalves, gastropods, crinoids, etc.
Tools: Geological hammer, short handle rake, spray bottle
Vehicle type: Good road. Any vehicle is OK.
Precautions and restrictions: Park well off the highway. Use flashers.
Accommodations: Meridian State Park is about 15 miles northwest of Clifton.
It takes around 15 minutes to drive the distance. They offer a variety of camping
opportunities. Quite a few sites are full hookup, which is water, electric, and sewer
hookups. They also offer water and electric sites as well as a primitive tenting area.

Image of site

Sites 22–27

Besides the state park, there are a lot of private campgrounds and RV parks in the area. Numerous hotels and motels are available in the area.

Meridian fossils

SPECIAL ATTRACTIONS

Meridian State Park offers good to fair fishing in their 72-acre lake. Access from the shore is possible, and they also have a barrier-free fishing pier for your convenience. You can also rent canoes and row boats. The lake has channel catfish, largemouth bass, white crappie, and carp, and it is stocked periodically with rainbow trout. Licenses are not needed in Texas state parks, and the park supplies loaner fishing tackle for fishing within the park.

Besides fishing, there are a number of fine hiking trails at the park. Another is birding, which has been becoming more and more popular all the time.

Bosque people from southern France and northern Spain were early settlers in the Clifton area. The Bosque Museum in downtown Clifton is dedicated to preserving the culture and artifacts of these folks. It is well worth a visit.

FINDING THE SITE

Meridian is a small city in Bosque County about 70 miles south of Fort Worth. It takes a little more than an hour to drive the distance. It is 46 miles from Waco, about an hour's drive. In the town of Meridian from the junction of Morgan Street and TX 22, travel east on TX 22 for 2.2 miles. This will take you just beyond a sign marking the town limits. Stop here.

ROCKHOUNDING

This area has an abundance of marine fossils that include but are not limited to bivalve clams, urchins, crinoids, and many others. The GPS numbers were taken at this stop but don't limit yourself to this area. There are fossils over a wide area in this region.

23. TX 22 Fossils aka Rudist Crystal Reef

Image of site

See map on page 58.
Land type: Lightly forested with ranches
GPS: 31.873258 / -97.4588454
Elevation: 581 feet
Best time of year: Fall, spring, and winter if there is no snow on the ground
Land manager: Texas Department of Transportation
Material: Marine fossils
Tools: Geological hammer, short handle rake, garden shovel, spray bottle
Vehicle type: Good highway. 2-wheel drive is OK.
Precautions and restrictions: Park well off the highway. Use flashers.
Accommodations: Meridian State Park is about 15 miles northwest of Clifton. It takes around 15 minutes to drive the distance. They offer a variety of camping opportunities. Quite a few sites are full hookup,which is water, electric, and sewer

hookups. They also offer water and electric sites as well as a primitive tenting area. Besides the state park, there are a lot of private campgrounds and RV parks in the area. Numerous hotels and motels are available in the area.

SPECIAL ATTRACTIONS

Meridian State Park offers good to fair fishing in their 72-acre lake. Access from the shore is possible, and they also have a barrier-free fishing pier for your convenience. You can also rent canoes and row boats. The lake has channel catfish, largemouth bass, white crappie, and carp, and it is stocked periodically with rainbow trout. Licenses are not needed in Texas state parks, and the park supplies loaner fishing tackle for fishing within the park.

Besides fishing, there are a number of fine hiking trails at the park. Another attraction is birding, which has been becoming more and more popular all the time.

Bosque people from southern France and northern Spain were early settlers in the Clifton area. The Bosque Museum in downtown Clifton is dedicated to preserving the culture and artifacts of these folks. It is well worth a visit.

FINDING THE SITE

Meridian is a small city in Bosque County about 70 miles south of Fort Worth. It takes a little more than an hour to drive the distance. It is 46 miles from Waco, about an hour's drive. In the town of Meridian from the junction of Morgan Street and TX 22 travel east on TX 22 and drive 12.4 miles.

ROCKHOUNDING

The Rudist Crystal Reef is well known in the fossil collecting world. This location boasts similar fossils to that of the Meridian site. These marine fossils include but are not limited to clams and other bivalves, urchins, crinoids, and others. Do not limit yourselves to this particular location. Fossils can be found on both sides of the road for a few miles from the junction of TX 22 and TX 219 along TX 22, both east and west of the junction.

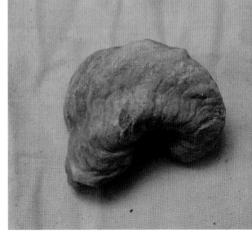

Typical fossil from TX 22

24. Clifton Fossils

Typical fossil rock of the area

See map on page 58.
Land type: Lightly forested; some farmland
GPS: 31.81508 / -97.6114183
Elevation: 673 feet
Best time of year: Spring and fall. it can be very hot in summer and cold in winter.
Land manager: Texas Department of Transportation
Material: Marine fossils
Tools: Geological hammer, short handle rake, garden shovel, spray bottle
Vehicle type: Good highway and side road. 2-wheel drive is sufficient.
Precautions and restrictions: Park well off the pavement. If you cannot, drive a little farther and walk back. Use your warning flashers.
Accommodations: Meridian State Park is about 15 miles northwest of Clifton. It takes around 15 minutes to drive the distance. They offer a variety of camping

opportunities. Quite a few sites are full hookup, which is water, electric, and sewer hookups. They also offer water and electric sites as well as a primitive tenting area. Besides the state park, there are a lot of private campgrounds and RV parks in the area. Numerous hotels and motels are available in the area.

SPECIAL ATTRACTIONS

Meridian State Park offers good to fair fishing in their 72-acre lake. Access from the shore is possible, and they also have a barrier-free fishing pier for your convenience. You can also rent canoes and row boats. The lake has channel catfish, largemouth bass, white crappie, and carp, and it is stocked periodically with rainbow trout. Licenses are not needed in Texas state parks, and the park supplies loaner fishing tackle for fishing within the park.

Besides fishing, there are a number of fine hiking trails at the park. Another attraction is birding, which has been becoming more and more popular all the time.

Bosque people from southern France and northern Spain were early settlers in the Clifton area. The Bosque Museum in downtown Clifton is dedicated to preserving the culture and artifacts of these folks. It is well worth a visit.

FINDING THE SITE

Clifton is the largest city in Bosque County, in Central Texas, and sits about 90 miles south of Fort Worth. It is about 35 miles from Waco with a drive of about 45 minutes. It takes about an hour and a half to drive there from the big city. From the junction of TX 6 and 5th Avenue in downtown Clifton, drive 3.1 miles on TX 6 to Texas Farm Road 3110, turn right (east), and travel 0.1 mile.

ROCKHOUNDING

This area's geology is composed primarily of Cretaceous limestone. These rocks, which were formed during that era under water, were eventually uplifted. This is what we see today. They are very fossiliferous. Almost every rock will have gastropods, urchins, corals, and bivalves. Some of the rocks are quite large and would be great for lining a garden. Drive the entire road and fossils will be found almost everywhere.

25. North of Mound Fossils

View from your vehicle

See map on page 58.
Land type: Lightly forested; some farmland
GPS: 31.388875 / -97.6228567
Elevation: 692 feet
Best time of year: Spring, late summer, autumn, and winter when snow free. It can be hot in summer and very cold in winter.
Land manager: Texas Department of Transportation
Material: Marine fossils
Tools: Geological hammer, short handle rake, stiff brush
Vehicle type: Good highway. Any vehicle would be OK.
Precautions and restrictions: Park well off the road. Folks appear to drive fast here. Use flashers. If you cannot park completely off the pavement, move down the road until you find an appropriate location and walk back.

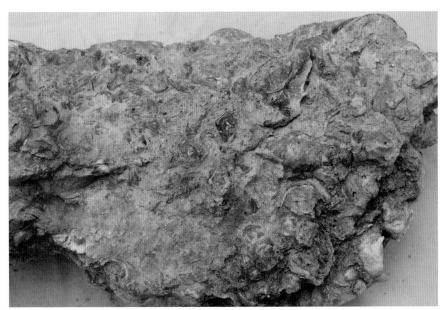

Fossils found north of Mound

Accommodations: This area is quite close to Mother Neff State Park in Moody. It is about 15 miles from there, and it takes about 15 minutes to drive the distance. This park offers full hookup sites as well as primitive tenting locations. There is a lodge present for the less adventuresome. In addition to the state park, there are a number of private RV resorts and campgrounds. A variety of motels can be found in the area.

SPECIAL ATTRACTIONS

Mother Neff State Park offers hiking, picnicking, geocaching, and nature observation. Enjoy the wildflowers in the prairie and explore the canyon trails. Swimming and fishing are not allowed.

Explore the interactive displays at their visitor center to learn more about this Central Texas treasure and its rich history.

There are nearly 3.5 miles of hiking trails for beginners to more experienced trekkers. Trails take you to Wash Pond, the CCC Rock Tower, and to a cave used by the Tonkawa Indian tribe in the 1800s.

FINDING THE SITE

Mound is an unincorporated community in Coryell County. It is about 90 miles north of Austin, and the drive takes about an hour and a half. From US

84 and Texas Farm Road 1829, drive south on Texas Farm Road 1829 for 2.3 miles where it joins Texas Farm Road 107 and continue on Texas Farm Road 107/1829 for 0.3 mile. At this point Texas Farm Road 1829 veers off to the left and Texas Farm Road 107 continues straight. At this junction you will see a big, couple-hundred-foot-long limestone cliff on the left. This is the fossil site.

ROCKHOUNDING

The underlying limestone in this area is not exposed a lot. Where it is, a large variety of marine fossils are evident. At those locations the fossils are very numerous. Ammonites, gastropods, urchins, and crinoids are in the rocks. The ammonites are not very abundant but present.

26. US 84 Picnic Area Fossils

In the rest area

See map on page 58.
Land type: Pine forest, ranches, and farms
GPS: 31.4733288 / -98.0388219
Elevation: 1,024 feet
Best time of year: Spring, late summer, fall, and winter when snow free. It can be cold in winter and very hot in summer.
Land manager: Texas Department of Transportation
Material: Marine fossils
Tools: Geological hammer, short handle rake
Vehicle type: Good highway. Any vehicle is OK.
Precautions and restrictions: Nice place to pull off the road. Park so that others can pass.

Fossils found here

Accommodations: For a different type of experience take a look at the Buena Vista Wildlife Safari and RV Park. They are set up for the entire family to experience an adventure. Adults can relax while the kids are off exploring the park. This facility boasts 34 RV sites all with full hookups. Each site is a paved driveway and most are pull through. The RV park is right next to the Wildlife Safari so you will have beautiful views from anywhere in the park. The kids can enjoy the playground and petting zoo while the entire family can participate in games at the Event Center. Cabins complete with all amenities are also available. There also are a number of other RV parks and campgrounds in the area. Motels are available in Evant or Arnett.

SPECIAL ATTRACTIONS

If you have time, a stop at the Coryell Museum and Historical Center in Gatesville is certainly worth your time. This institution has a very attractive collection of local historical artifacts and documents. The museum's primary purpose is to collect, preserve, and display artifacts related to the settling and building of Central Texas, from the days of the Republic of Texas to today. Also included in the collections are a number of fossils that were found locally. It can give you an idea of what you might run across rockhounding around this location.

Table and bench constructed of flint nodules

The museum also has a restaurant that has received high praise in many reviews.

FINDING THE SITE

This site is about 70 miles west of Waco. It is about 7 miles east of Evant on US 84 and 9.4 miles west of Arnett. From Evant at the junction of US 84 and US 281, drive 6.5 miles east on US 84 to the picnic area on the south side.

ROCKHOUNDING

This area sits on Cretaceous rocks. You will find eroded limestone with some fossils here. Material is not very abundant but available. Take a look at the stone picnic table. Someone constructed the legs of the stools incorporating agate and flint nodules. It is a very attractive piece of stone art. Be sure to check out the road cuts on the 6.5 miles back to Evant.

27. South of Evant, US 281 Fossils

Numerous fossils in road cut

See map on page 58.
Land type: Pine forest and ranch land
GPS: 31.4566357 / -98.167904
Elevation: 1,265 feet
Best time of year: Spring, late summer, fall, and winter when snow free. It can be cold in winter and very hot in summer.
Land manager: Texas Department of Transportation
Material: Small marine fossils in hard limestone
Tools: Geological hammer, short handle rake, garden shovel, spray bottle
Vehicle type: Good highway. 2-wheel drive is sufficient.
Precautions and restrictions: Nice place to pull off the road. Park so that others can pass.
Accommodations: For a different type of experience take a look at the Buena Vista Wildlife Safari and RV Park. They are set up for the entire family to experience

Looking over what's available

an adventure. Adults can relax while the kids are off exploring the park. This facility boosts 34 RV sites all with full hookups. Each site is a paved driveway and most are pull through. The RV park is right next to the Wildlife Safari, so you will have beautiful views from anywhere in the park. The kids can enjoy the playground and petting zoo while the entire family can participate in games at the Event Center. Cabins complete with all amenities are also available. There also are a number of other RV parks and campgrounds in the area. Motels are available in Evant or Arnett.

SPECIAL ATTRACTIONS

If you have time, a stop at the Coryell Museum and Historical Center in Gatesville is certainly worth your time. This institution has a very attractive collection of local historical artifacts and documents. The museum's primary purpose is to collect, preserve, and display artifacts related to the settling and building of Central Texas, from the days of the Republic of Texas to today. Also included in the collections are a number of fossils that were found locally. It can give you an idea of what you might run across rockhounding in and

Typical fossils at south of Evant

around this location. The museum also has a restaurant that has received high praise in many reviews.

FINDING THE SITE

Evant is a town in Coryell and Hamilton Counties in Central Texas. It is about 100 miles from Austin and takes around an hour and a half to drive there. From Evant travel south on US 281. Just past the Buena Vista Wildlife Safari sign on the right, turn into a small picnic area on the west side of the road. You drive at an incline into the picnic area.

ROCKHOUNDING

There are small marine fossils embedded in the cliff wall. We are not sure if they were placed there for everyone to enjoy, but it would probably be better to leave them be instead of chiseling. There are some small pieces to be picked up.

28. Lampasas Marine Fossils

Land type: Pine forest and ranch land
GPS: 31.0351283 / -98.1485083
Elevation: 1,037 feet
Best time of year: Spring, late summer, fall, and winter when snow free. It can be cold in winter and very hot in summer.
Land manager: Texas Department of Transportation
Material: Marine fossils including oysters and root castings
Tools: Geological hammer, short handle rake, garden shovel, spray bottle
Vehicle type: Good highway. 2-wheel drive is sufficient.
Precautions and restrictions: Be sure to park completely off the pavement. If you cannot do so at the location, it is better to drive a little farther until you find a spot where you can and walk back. Be sure to use your warning flashers upon stopping.
Accommodations: Colorado Bend State Park is about 27 miles west of Lampasas. It is a 40-minute drive. This is one of Texas's most remote parks. It offers

Image of site

Sites 28–45

Typical fossil stone from Lampasas

back-to-nature camping with drive-up sites as well as hike-in sites. These camping locations have water but no electric hookups nor sewer hookups. Composting toilets are near the main camping area and at one trailhead. An open-air, rinse-off shower is near the campground. There also are a number of commercial RV parks and campgrounds in the area. Motels are available along the main roads.

SPECIAL ATTRACTIONS

Colorado Bend State Park sports 35 miles of hiking trails. These range from easy to very difficult. One of the favorites is Gorman Falls Hike. Take a self-guided tour to this 70-foot spring-fed waterfall. Come prepared for a 3-mile round-trip hike over rough and rocky terrain. Folks who spend time here also paddle and swim in the river. Fishing is good especially in the spring when the white bass run up the river to spawn.

Copper Spring Nature Park was named for the natural spring on the property. It is composed of 23 acres dedicated to the preservation and encouragement of wildlife. The most popular feature of the park is the series of trails. Invasive plants had been a problem in the past but volunteers have cleared them out and planted native varieties to create a space welcoming to birds and butterflies as well as humans. There is no charge to enjoy this refreshing slice of nature in downtown Lampasas. It has been a labor of love that volunteers have maintained. Located on Hackberry Street between Avenue A and 2nd Street.

FINDING THE SITE

Lampasas is a city in Lampasas County. It is about 70 miles north-northwest of Austin. The drive from the big city takes about 1 hour and 15 minutes. From south of Lampasas at the junction of US 281 and US 183 go south on US 183 for 4.4 miles. There will be a ledge on the right (west) side of the road.

ROCKHOUNDING

This site has Cretaceous fossils, which are composed of primarily oysters and root castings. Pennsylvanian and Mississippian fossils should not be ruled out as there are some rocks from those periods nearby. Do not confine yourselves to this site at these GPS numbers. There are many other locations in the general area. In fact you can find these rocks almost anywhere within a few miles of these GPS numbers.

29. Colorado River Fossils

The pretty Colorado River

See map on page 74.
Land type: Very lightly forested and hilly
GPS: 31.0889471 / -98.5220602
Elevation: 1,106 feet
Best time of year: Spring, late summer, fall, and winter when snow free. It can be cold in winter and very hot in summer.
Land manager: Texas Department of Transportation
Material: Pennsylvanian marine fossils, jasper, flint
Tools: Geological hammer, garden shovel, stiff brush, various sizes of flathead screwdrivers
Vehicle type: Good road. 2-wheel drive is sufficient.
Precautions and restrictions: Park well out of the way of other vehicles.
Accommodations: Colorado Bend State Park is about 27 miles west of Lampasas. It is a 40-minute drive. This is one of Texas's most remote parks. It offers

The Colorado River at this site

back-to-nature camping with drive-up sites as well as hike-in sites. These camping locations have water but no electric hookups nor sewer hookups. Composting toilets are near the main camping area and at one trailhead. An open-air, rinse-off shower is near the campground. There also are a number of commercial RV parks and campgrounds in the area. Motels are available along the main roads.

SPECIAL ATTRACTIONS

Colorado Bend State Park sports 35 miles of hiking trails. These range from easy to very difficult. One of the favorites is Gorman Falls Hike. Take a self-guided tour to this 70-foot spring-fed waterfall. Come prepared for a 3-mile round-trip hike over rough and rocky terrain. Folks who spend time here also paddle and swim in the river. Fishing is good especially in the spring when the white bass run up the river to spawn.

Sulphur Spring Camp is a top attraction in this area. Here the great outdoors of Texas Hill Country can be appreciated. Most folks come here to go fishing. The Colorado River provides all types of fish including perch, flathead, stripers, catfish, carp, crappie, buffalo, gar, sand bass, and white bass. Wildlife observation is also a popular activity. Besides these activities, the camp

Typical fossils at the Colorado River

also offers swimming, bird watching, volleyball, inner tubing, and white-water canoeing. RV as well as tent sites are available.

FINDING THE SITE

Bend is an unincorporated community in Lampasas and San Saba Counties in western Central Texas. It is about 90 miles northwest of Austin, and the drive time is about 1 hour and 45 minutes. Coming into the small town of Bend on Texas Farm Road 580 from the east, at downtown Bend, Texas Farm Road 580 makes a sharp right-hand turn. From that point drive 0.9 mile. There is a fenced-in area with an open cast-iron gate. Turn right and drive down a black shale road to the river to a parking area.

ROCKHOUNDING

The fossils are encased between the layers of the shale. This place is for serious fossil hunters only. It does take some time and effort to split them open. This rock is from the Smithwick Formation of the Pennsylvanian Era. Included in the assortment found here are trilobites, cephalopods, and gastropods. We also found some nice pieces of flint lying around as float.

30. Bend Flint and Jasper

Image of site

See map on page 74.
Land type: Forested and quite hilly
GPS: 31. 0838655 / -98.5312207
Elevation: 1,253 feet
Best time of year: Spring, summer, autumn, and winter when not snow covered. It can be quite cold in the winter.
Land manager: Texas Department of Transportation
Material: Flint, jasper, agate
Tools: Geological hammer, short handle rake, garden shovel, spray bottle
Vehicle type: Good road. Any vehicle is OK.
Precautions and restrictions: It was a bit tough to park here. If you drive just past the location, there is a better place to pull off the road. Use your flashers.
Accommodations: Colorado Bend State Park is about 27 miles west of Lampasas. It is a 40-minute drive. This is one of Texas's most remote parks. It offers

back-to-nature camping with drive-up sites as well as hike-in sites. These camping locations have water but no electric hookups nor sewer hookups. Composting toilets are near the main camping area and at one trailhead. An open-air, rinse-off shower is near the campground. There also are a number of commercial RV parks and campgrounds in the area. Motels are available along the main roads.

SPECIAL ATTRACTIONS

Colorado Bend State Park sports 35 miles of hiking trails. These range from easy to very difficult. One of the favorites is Gorman Falls Hike. Take a self-guided tour to this 70-foot spring-fed waterfall. Come prepared for a 3-mile round-trip hike over rough and rocky terrain. Folks who spend time here also paddle and swim in the river. Fishing is good especially in the spring when the white bass run up the river to spawn.

Pretty Bend flint

Sulphur Spring Camp is a top attraction in this area. Here the great outdoors of Texas Hill Country can be appreciated. Most folks come here to go fishing. The Colorado River provides all types of fish including perch, flathead, stripers, catfish, carp, crappie, buffalo, gar, sand bass, and white bass. Wildlife observation is also a popular activity. Besides these activities, the camp also offers swimming, bird watching, volleyball, inner tubing, and white-water canoeing. RV as well as tent sites are available.

Pretty Bend flint

FINDING THE SITE

Bend is an unincorporated community in Lampasas and San Saba Counties in western Central Texas. It is about 90 miles northwest of Austin and the drive

Plentiful material here

time is about 1 hour and 45 minutes. From downtown Bend continue west on Texas Farm Road 580 to its junction with Texas Farm Road 501. Turn west onto Texas Farm Road 501 and continue 0.2 mile to a hillside on the right.

ROCKHOUNDING

There is a lot of material here, but much of it has a very weathered exterior. Each piece must be chipped to see what is inside. Almost all the pieces we cracked were either flint, agate, or jasper in a variety of colors and patterns. All were very attractive. Do not limit yourselves to this location. The area has an abundance of nice material. Make other stops along the way.

31. Cherokee Patterned Chalcedony

See map on page 74.
Land type: Pine forests and ranch land
GPS: 30.9815212 / -98.6305458
Elevation: 920 feet
Best time of year: Spring and fall
Land manager: Texas Department of Transportation
Material: Flint, agate, and petrified wood
Tools: Geological hammer, short handle rake, garden shovel, spray bottle
Vehicle type: Good highway. 2-wheel drive is sufficient.
Precautions and restrictions: Parking can be tight. Pull well off the pavement. If you cannot pull off the pavement, drive on until you can and walk back. Use your warning flashers.

The roadside location at Cherokee

Accommodations: Colorado Bend State Park is about 27 miles west of Lampasas. It is a 40-minute drive. This is one of Texas's most remote parks. It offers back-to-nature camping with drive-up sites as well as hike-in sites. These camping locations have water but no electric hookups nor sewer hookups. Composting toilets are near the main camping area and at one trailhead. An open-air, rinse-off shower is near the campground. There also are a number of commercial RV parks and campgrounds in the area. Motels are available along the main roads.

SPECIAL ATTRACTIONS

The San Saba Nature Park is certainly worth the visit. It is about 15 miles and

The roadside location at Cherokee   Lots of pretty chalcedony here

a 15-minute drive from Cherokee. The park boasts a fine walking trail with informational signs along the way. These signs are a combination of history and nature related. The park itself is dedicated to history, bird watching, river walking, and nature observing. There are about 3 miles of trails, and folks can spend an entire day participating in all that it has to offer.

FINDING THE SITE

Cherokee is an unincorporated community in San Saba County in western Central Texas. It is about 90 miles northwest of Austin with a drive time of 1 hour and 45 minutes. From the junction of TX 16 and Texas Farm Road 501, head northeast on Texas Farm Road 501 for 4.6 miles. You will see a road cut on the north side of the highway.

ROCKHOUNDING

There are many flint and jasper stones, but one can find the patterned stones by putting in enough time and effort. We only found small tumblers. To find larger pieces, digging is necessary. It could be worth the effort because this material is very attractive.

32. Llanite Granite

These boulders comprise mostly llanite.

See map on page 74.
Land type: Rolling hills, grass lands, and ranches
GPS: 30.8904565 / -98.6585694
Elevation: 1,123 feet
Best time of year: Late spring, summer, and early fall. We were there in the winter and it was fine, but can be snow covered at times.
Land manager: Texas Department of Transportation
Material: Llanite and other granite
Tools: For smaller pieces: geological hammer, short handle rake, garden shovel, spray bottle; for larger chunks: gads, chisels, crowbars, sledgehammer, safety glasses, heavy duty gloves, respirator, and lots of strong arm muscles
Vehicle type: Good highway. 2-wheel drive is sufficient
Precautions and restrictions: Can be tight parking. Be sure you are parked well off the pavement. If this is not possible, drive ahead and find an appropriate spot to pull off. Walk back to the boulders. Use your warning flashers.

Notice the blue crystals in the rock.

Accommodations: Llano City Park has full hookups, pull-through sites, and back-in sites. It has all the amenities, and at the time of this writing was very reasonable. It includes 30- or 50-amp service, water and sewer hookups, picnic tables, showers, laundry, and Wi-Fi. This is a lovely spot overlooking the river where one can walk and possibly find pieces of llanite or other granites as well as flint, jasper, and agates. Also located in Llano are Badu Park and Grenwelge Park, which are run by the county. Badu Park also offers RV campsites.

SPECIAL ATTRACTIONS

Enchanted Rock Natural Area is a must-see if you are in the area. It sits about 25 miles north-northeast of Llano. It takes about a half an hour to drive the distance.

The massive pink granite dome rising above Central Texas has inspired many mystical legends about its ability to change people's lives. The rock has drawn people for thousands of years. The Natural Area is more than just the dome. The scenery, rock formations, and legends are magical, too. The area sports 11 miles of hiking trails, and rock climbing is a popular pastime here.

Notice the blue crystals in the rock.

FINDING THE SITE

Llano is about 75 miles northwest of Austin and it takes about an hour and a quarter to drive the distance. From Llano at the junction of TX 16 and E. Young Street, go north on TX 16 for 9.4 miles. You will find a very distinctive large road cut on both sides. The east side is bigger and more obvious.

ROCKHOUNDING

Llanite appears to be like any other granite, but upon close examination there are beautiful blue quartz crystals that shine through the feldspar and look like liquid. It has been said that this is the only world location for this type of granite. Each stone has a different combination of quartz and feldspar.

Llanite takes a great polish and has been used to make beautiful bookends, spheres, and cubes. It also produces very attractive cabs to be made into pendants, earrings, bolo ties, and so on.

To obtain large pieces one must put in a lot of effort chiseling with gads and prying pieces off. However, there are many smaller pieces lying around as float or that can be found by sifting through the tailings left by others.

33. Llano River Flint and Llanite

The bridge over the Llano River

See map on page 74.
Land type: City with some forest
GPS: 30.7514537 / -98.6745955
Elevation: 996 feet
Best time of year: Summer, spring, fall
Land manager: The City of Llano
Material: Flint, jasper, granite, llanite
Tools: Geological hammer, short handle rake, garden shovel, spray bottle
Vehicle type: Good road to the beginning of the path down to river. 2-wheel drive is OK.
Precautions and restrictions: The path down to the river as well as the river rocks can be slippery.
Accommodations: Llano City Park has full hookups, pull-through sites, and back-in sites. It has all the amenities, and at the time of this writing was very reasonable.

It includes 30- or 50-amp service, water and sewer hookups, picnic tables, showers, laundry, and Wi-Fi. This is a lovely spot overlooking the river where one can walk and possibly find pieces of llanite or other granites as well as flint, jasper, and agates. Also located in Llano are Badu Park and Grenwelge Park, which are run by the county. Badu Park also offers RV campsites.

A nice variety of chalcedony from the Llano River

SPECIAL ATTRACTIONS

Enchanted Rock Natural Area is a must-see if you are in the area. It sits about 25 miles north-northeast of Llano. It takes about a half an hour to drive the distance.

The massive pink granite dome rising above Central Texas has inspired many mystical legends about its ability to change people's lives. The rock has drawn people for thousands of years. The Natural Area is more than just the dome. The scenery, rock formations, and legends are magical, too. The area sports 11 miles of hiking trails, and rock climbing is a popular pastime here.

FINDING THE SITE

Llano is about 75 miles northwest of Austin and it takes about an hour and a quarter to drive the distance. At the south end of the bridge crossing the Llano River, turn east onto Hayne Street. Drive past the public bathroom and park in the parking area of Grenwelge Park.

ROCKHOUNDING

From the parking area, follow the trail down to the river. You will find a lot of flint and jasper along the path's sides. When the river bars are accessible, many pieces of chalcedony as well as llanite and other attractive granites can be gathered. When we were there, the river was high and as a result the banks and bar were covered with water.

34. Marble Falls Chalcedony

The site from across the road

See map on page 74.
Land type: Rolling hills, forested
GPS: 30.5354667 / -98.2521483
Elevation: 823 feet
Best time of year: Summer, spring, fall
Land manager: Texas Department of Transportation
Material: Agate, jasper, flint
Tools: Geological hammer, short handle rake, garden shovel, spray bottle
Vehicle type: Good road all the way to site. 2-wheel drive is sufficient.
Precautions and restrictions: Can be tight parking. Be sure you are parked well off the pavement. If this is not possible, drive ahead and find an appropriate spot to pull off. Walk back to the site. Use your warning flashers.
Accommodations: The site is about 35 miles away from Pedernales Falls State Park and takes about 40 minutes to drive the distance. This park offers a fine

camping experience. There are
sites with water and electricity as
well as hike-in tent campsites. A
group campsite is also available.
Besides the park, there are
many private RV parks and
campgrounds in the area. Motels
will be found throughout the
region especially in Johnson City.

Nice flint and agate from the Marble Falls site

SPECIAL ATTRACTIONS

Pedernales Falls State Park offers some beautiful hiking and biking trails. The
trail difficulty ranges from easy at the 0.5-mile Twin Falls Nature Trail to the
challenging Wolf Mountain Trail, which runs for 6 miles. The challenging
Wolf Mountain Trail circumnavigates both Wolf and Tobacco Mountains. It
winds its way along the small canyons created by Mescal and Tobacco Creeks.

The park also offers paddling in the river as well as swimming off the
beach at Trammell's Crossing Trail.

Horseback riding is a popular activity at the park, and all the infrastructure to facilitate this is present.

Don't miss the Falls exhibit at the Colorado Museum in Marble Falls.
They have displays on the history and geology of Marble Falls.

FINDING THE SITE

Mable Falls is a city in Burnet County. It is about 49 miles northwest of Austin,
and it takes about 1 hour and 10 minutes to drive the distance. From US 281
after crossing the Colorado River, continue 1.1 miles to Texas Farm Road
2147. Turn east (left) and drive to the road cut. Be careful because the Texas
Farm Road 2147 west is immediately to the right after crossing the river. To
get to the eastbound section of the road, you have to drive another 1.1 miles.

ROCKHOUNDING

We originally found this site while looking for another that was not found. In
fact, like a number of other sites listed in old books, there was a house sitting
right on the location. So we decided to make a random stop and immediately found material. Most of it was colorful float, but some careful scraping
exposed a few larger pieces.

35. Johnson City Flint

The road cut containing abundant material

See map on page 74.
Land type: Pine forests and residential
GPS: 30.315855 / -98.39105
Elevation: 1,198 feet
Best time of year: All year except when there is snow on the ground
Land manager: Texas Department of Transportation
Material: Patterned flint
Tools: Geological hammer, short handle rake, garden shovel, spray bottle
Vehicle type: Good highway. 2-wheel drive is sufficient.
Precautions and restrictions: Parking can be tight. This is a very busy road so pull well off the pavement. If you cannot pull off the pavement, drive on until you can and walk back. Use your warning flashers.
Accommodations: The site is about 13 miles away from Pedernales Falls State Park. This park offers a fine camping experience. There are sites with water and

electricity as well as hike-in tent campsites. A group campsite is also available. Besides the park, there are many private RV parks and campgrounds in the area. Motels will be found throughout the region especially in Johnson City.

SPECIAL ATTRACTIONS

Pedernales Falls State Park offers some beautiful hiking and biking trails. The trail difficulty ranges from easy at the 0.5-mile Twin Falls Nature Trail to the challenging Wolf Mountain Trail, which runs for 6 miles. The challenging Wolf Mountain Trail circumnavigates both Wolf and Tobacco Mountains. It winds its way along the small canyons created by Mescal and Tobacco Creeks.

The park also offers paddling in the river as well as swimming off the beach at Trammell's Crossing Trail.

Horseback riding is a popular activity at the park, and all the infrastructure to facilitate this is present.

If you happen to be in the area toward the end of August, be sure to check out the Blanco County Fair and Rodeo. It is a real fun time for the entire family.

Flint in a variety of colors from this site

FINDING THE SITE

Johnson City is a city in and the county seat of Blanco County. The city is about 50 miles west of Austin with a drive time of about 50 minutes. It sits about 65 miles north of San Antonio, and it takes about 1 hour and 15 minutes to drive the distance. From Johnson City at the junction of US 281 and US 290, drive north on US 281 for 2.9 miles. You will be at a large exposed road cut on both sides of the highway. Pull off the road here.

ROCKHOUNDING

The flint here is quite attractive. The colors range from white to velvety brown. The most attractive pieces are mixtures of both. Some pieces include lines of clear and white quartz. You will find small pieces on the ground, but the best have to be chiseled out of the wall. The chiseling is not too difficult.

Some pieces, upon first glance, appear that they would not polish very well because of the texture. Don't be fooled. When polished, this material becomes very attractive with the white floating above the brown with lines of quartz passing through.

36. Stonewall City Flint

View of collecting location from road

See map on page 74.
Land type: Hilly pine forests and ranch land
GPS: 30.2386689 / -98.5934132
Elevation: 1,468 feet
Best time of year: All year except when snow is on the ground. It can be very cold in the winter.
Land manager: Texas Department of Transportation
Material: Flint, some agate
Tools: Geological hammer, short handle rake, garden shovel, spray bottle
Vehicle type: Good highway. 2-wheel drive is sufficient.
Precautions and restrictions: Parking can be tight. This can be a busy road so pull well off the pavement. If you cannot pull off the pavement, drive on until you can and walk back. Use your warning flashers.

Accommodations: The site is about 13 miles away from Pedernales Falls State Park. This park offers a fine camping experience. There are sites with water and electricity as well as hike-in tent campsites. A group campsite is also available. Besides the park, there are many private RV parks and campgrounds in the area. Motels will be found throughout the region especially in Johnson City.

SPECIAL ATTRACTIONS

Pedernales Falls State Park offers some beautiful hiking and biking trails. The trail difficulty ranges from easy at the 0.5-mile Twin Falls Nature Trail to the challenging Wolf Mountain Trail, which runs for 6 miles. The challenging Wolf Mountain Trail circumnavigates both Wolf and Tobacco Mountains. It winds its way along the small canyons created by Mescal and Tobacco Creeks.

The park also offers paddling in the river as well as swimming off the beach at Trammell's Crossing Trail.

Horseback riding is a popular activity at the park, and all the infrastructure to facilitate this is present.

FINDING THE SITE

Stonewall is an unincorporated community and census-designated place in Gillespie County. It is about 65 miles west of Austin with a drive time of 1 hour and 15 minutes. Stonewall is also located about 70 miles north of San Antonio, and it takes about 1 hour and 15 minutes to drive the distance. Traveling west from Johnson City on US 290 from its junction with US 281, at 11.9 miles there is an area of erosion on the right side. This is the location.

An interesting piece of petrified wood from Stonewall

ROCKHOUNDING

This is Gillespie County flint and some of the finest flint available in Texas. Some of the gray flint contains areas of tan, pink, brown, and white. In the mix, a few agates can be located. A good quantity can be picked up off the ground, but digging may produce larger specimens.

37. Fredericksburg Flint and Agate

See map on page 74.
Land type: Lightly wooded and ranch land
GPS: 30.3423517 / -98.8577367
Elevation: 1,823 feet
Best time of year: Spring, early summer, late summer, fall. It may be snow covered in winter but otherwise OK. Midsummer is also OK, but it can be very hot.
Land manager: Texas Department of Transportation
Material: Flint and agate
Tools: Geological hammer, short handle rake, garden shovel, spray bottle
Vehicle type: Good road all the way. 2-wheel drive is sufficient.
Precautions and restrictions: Parking can be tight. Pull well off the pavement. If you cannot pull off the pavement, drive on until you can and walk back. Use your warning flashers.
Accommodations: Fredericksburg is about 43 miles away from Pedernales Falls State Park. It takes about 51 minutes to drive there. This park offers a fine camping experience. There are sites with water and electricity as well as hike-in tent campsites. A group campsite is also available. Besides the park, there are many private RV parks and campgrounds in the area. Motels and hotels will be found in Fredericksburg and throughout the region.

Be careful to park well off the road here.

An attractive piece of Fredericksburg petrified wood

SPECIAL ATTRACTIONS

Enchanted Rock is close by. It is a 500-foot dome of granite. Lots of folks like to climb it. Native Americans thought of this rock as having special powers.

Fredericksburg was originally settled by German immigrants. It still maintains that flavor. There are a variety of German restaurants and German places. When entering the town, the sign says "Willkommen," which translates to "Welcome" in English.

FINDING THE SITE

Fredericksburg is about 78 miles west of Austin with a drive time of about an hour and a half. The city is about 70 miles north-northwest of San Antonio. It takes about 1 hour and 10 minutes to drive the distance. In Fredericksburg, from the junction of US 87 and Texas Farm Road 965, travel 5 miles north on Texas Farm Road 965 to a large pull-off on the east side. This is a good pullout next to a large gravelly area.

ROCKHOUNDING

This flint is typical of Gillespie County. It is mostly gray but some pieces have variations resulting in very interesting cabs. Agate is also present in limited quantities. This collecting continues for another 10 miles. You will probably find material at any pullout.

38. US 87 Agate and Flint

Lots of material here

See map on page 74.
Land type: Hilly forested land with some residential development
GPS: 30.3560075 / -98.9244962
Elevation: 2,066 feet
Best time of year: Spring, early summer, late summer, fall
Land manager: Texas Department of Transportation
Material: Agate, flint, petrified wood
Tools: Geological hammer, long handle rake, garden shovel, spray bottle
Vehicle type: Paved road. 2-wheel drive is sufficient.
Precautions and restrictions: Parking can be tight. Pull well off the pavement. If you cannot pull off the pavement, drive on until you can and walk back. Use your warning flashers.

A nice variety of chalcedony can be collected here.

Accommodations: Fredericksburg is about 43 miles away from Pedernales Falls State Park. It takes about 51 minutes to drive there. This park offers a fine camping experience. There are sites with water and electricity as well as hike-in tent campsites. A group campsite is also available. Besides the park, there are many private RV parks and campgrounds in the area. Motels will be found throughout the region especially in the city of Fredericksburg.

SPECIAL ATTRACTIONS

Enchanted Rock Natural Area is a must-see if you are in the area. It sits about 17 miles north of Fredericksburg on Texas Farm Road 965. It takes about 20 minutes to drive the distance.

The massive pink granite dome rising above Central Texas has inspired many mystical legends about its ability to change people's lives. The rock has drawn people for thousands of years. The Natural Area is more than just the dome. The scenery, rock formations, and legends are magical, too. The area sports 11 miles of hiking trails, and rock climbing is a popular pastime here.

Fredericksburg was the second German town in Texas founded by the Adelsverein, better known as the Society for the Protection of German

A nice variety of chalcedony can be collected here.

Immigrants, on May 8, 1846. That rich history is still influential. The German origins of Fredericksburg are evident all over the city. There are lots of restaurants specializing in dishes of the old country. There's a German Cultural Center, and a sign as you enter the town says "Willkommen."

FINDING THE SITE
Fredericksburg is about 78 miles west of Austin with a drive time of about an hour and a half. The city is about 70 miles north-northwest of San Antonio. It takes about 1 hour and 10 minutes to drive that distance. From the junction of TX 16 and US 87 in Fredericksburg, continue northwest on US 87 to a road cut on the right side.

ROCKHOUNDING
This location contains both agate and flint. Much can be picked up off the ground, but digging usually produces more. Don't just stop here. If you are serious about rockhounding when you visit, make additional stops along the way.

39. US 87 Picture Rock

Look for area of white in the road cut.

See map on page 74.
Land type: Hilly forested land with some residential development
GPS: 30.14224941 / -98.972974
Elevation: 2,203 feet
Best time of year: Spring and early summer, late summer and fall. It may be snow covered in winter but otherwise OK.
Land manager: Texas Department of Transportation
Material: Picture rock
Tools: For small pieces: geological hammer, short handle rake, garden shovel, spray bottle; for larger chunks: gads, sledgehammers, chisels, crowbars, and a lot of upper body strength
Vehicle type: Good road. 2-wheel drive is sufficient.
Precautions and restrictions: Parking can be tight. Pull well off the pavement. If you cannot pull off the pavement, drive on until you can and walk back. Use your warning flashers.

Accommodations: Fredericksburg is about 43 miles away from Pedernales Falls State Park. It takes about 501 minutes to drive there. This park offers a fine camping experience. There are sites with water and electricity as well as hike-in tent campsites. A group campsite is also available. Besides the park, there are many private RV parks and campgrounds in the area. Motels will be found throughout the region especially in the city of Fredericksburg.

SPECIAL ATTRACTIONS

Enchanted Rock Natural Area is a must-see if you are in the area. It sits about 17 miles north of Fredericksburg on Texas Farm Road 965. It takes about 20 minutes to drive the distance.

The massive pink granite dome rising above Central Texas has inspired many mystical legends about its ability to change people's lives. The rock has drawn people for thousands of years. The Natural Area is more than just the dome. The scenery, rock formations, and legends are magical, too. The area sports 11 miles of hiking trails, and rock climbing is a popular pastime here.

Sandy picture rock

Fredericksburg was the second German town in Texas founded by the Adelsverein, better known as the Society for the Protection of German Immigrants, on May 8, 1846. That rich history is still influential. The German origins of Fredericksburg are evident all over the city. There are lots of restaurants specializing in dishes of the old country. There's a German Cultural Center, and a sign as you enter the town says "Willkommen."

FINDING THE SITE

Fredericksburg is about 78 miles west of Austin with a drive time of about an hour and a half. The city is about 70 miles north-northwest of San Antonio. It takes about 1 hour and 10 minutes to drive the distance. From the junction of TX 16 and US 87, drive 12.4 miles north to a very large high road cut on both sides. The road cut is a white wall below and dark rock above.

ROCKHOUNDING

While driving along, we just happened to be passing through this road cut. The white and dark combination was very striking, so we stopped to take a look around. What a surprise! In the erosional debris at the base of a cliff, a very attractive picture rock was found. This variety of scenic stones is actually limestone. It would make attractive large pieces like book ends. They also would be great garden liners.

40. Mason Quartz

This quartz tumbles nicely.

See map on page 74.
Land type: Rolling hills, forested ranch land
GPS: 30.8146114 / -99.2627617
Elevation: 1,769 feet
Best time of year: Spring and early summer, late summer and fall. It may be snow covered in winter but otherwise OK.
Land manager: Texas Department of Transportation
Material: White and clear quartz
Tools: Geological hammer, short handle rake, garden shovel, spray bottle
Vehicle type: Good highway all the way. 2-wheel drive is sufficient.
Precautions and restrictions: Parking can be tight. Pull well off the pavement. If you cannot pull off the pavement, drive on until you can and walk back. Use your warning flashers.

Accommodations: The South Llano River State Park is about 50 miles southwest of Mason. It takes about 50 minutes to drive the distance. They offer a variety of campsites. Most campsites have water and electric hookups and a restroom with showers nearby. The 6 walk-in sites have water and a restroom with showers nearby, while the 5 primitive hike-in sites have a chemical toilet nearby, but no water. In Mason, the city runs an RV park with 29 spaces. Some are pull-through while others are back-in. There is 30- and 50-amp electric service at all sites and some are full hookup. The cost for camping is reasonable.

SPECIAL ATTRACTIONS

The South Llano River State Park offers a lot of activities. Fishing is one of the most popular, and they do have tackle to lend for use within the park. No license is necessary if fishing within the state park.

Floating and paddling the river are popular activities as well. Kayaks and canoes are available and can be rented for a modest fee.

Nature watching and birding are also very popular. They offer birding blinds, and more than 250 species have been identified over the years at this park.

In Mason, the Mason Square Museum is definitely worth a visit. It is packed with old artifacts and displays the largest topaz ever found in Texas.

FINDING THE SITE

Mason is about 110 miles west of Austin and it takes about 2 hours to drive the distance. It is about 112 miles from San Antonio with a 1 hour and 50 minute drive time. From the junction of US 87 and TX 29 in Mason continue north on US 87 for 5.1 miles to a large road cut on the right. This is the location.

ROCKHOUNDING

The material here is white and clear quartz. There is some massive smoky in the mix. We include some quartz in every barrel that is tumbled. Often, the results are surprisingly attractive. Some of the pieces after tumbling display internal rainbows, which result from internal fractures. We never would have discovered some of these lovely pieces if they had not been tumbled. Of course, a lot is just left around to line the path at the old homestead.

41. Mason Flint Nodules and Picture Rock

Flint nodules exposed by erosion

See map on page 74.
Land type: Lightly forested and hilly
GPS: 30.8381067 / -99.2658017
Elevation: 1,993 feet
Best time of year: Spring, early summer, late summer, fall. It may be snow covered in winter but otherwise OK.
Land manager: Texas Department of Transportation
Material: Agate and flint nodules, picture rock
Tools: Geological hammer, short handle rake, garden shovel, and spray bottle for the pieces lying around. To extract more complete specimens from the wall, you will need gads, crowbars, sledgehammer, and chisel.
Vehicle type: Good highway all the way. 2-wheel drive is sufficient.
Precautions and restrictions: Parking can be tight. Pull well off the pavement. If you cannot pull off the pavement, drive on until you can and walk back. Use your warning flashers.

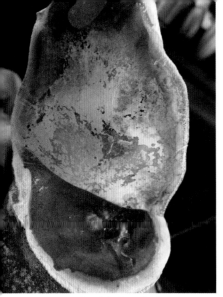
Typical nodule from this location

Accommodations: The South Llano River State Park is about 50 miles southwest of Mason. It takes about 50 minutes to drive the distance. They offer a variety of campsites. Most campsites have water and electric hookups, and a restroom with showers nearby. The 6 walk-in sites have water and a restroom with showers nearby, while the 5 primitive hike-in sites have a chemical toilet nearby, but no water. In Mason the city runs an RV park with 29 spaces. Some are pull-through while others are back-in. There is 30- and 50-amp electric service at all sites and some are full hookup.

SPECIAL ATTRACTIONS

The South Llano River State Park offers a lot of activities. Fishing is one of the most popular, and they do have tackle to lend for use within the park. No license is necessary if fishing within the park.

Floating and paddling the river are popular activities as well. Kayaks and canoes are available and can be rented for a modest fee.

Nature watching and birding are also very popular. They offer birding blinds, and over 250 species have been identified over the years at this park.

In Mason, the Mason Square Museum is definitely worth a visit. It is packed with old artifacts and displays the largest topaz ever found in Texas.

FINDING THE SITE

Mason is about 110 miles west of Austin and it takes about 2 hours to drive the distance. It is about 112 miles from San Antonio with a 1 hour and 50 minute drive time. From the junction of US 87 and TX 29 in the town of Mason, drive north on US 87 for 6.8 miles to a road cut on both sides.

ROCKHOUNDING

You will notice flint nodules lying around that have eroded out of the road cut. Chip the stones to reveal what is inside. We found a very pretty chocolate brown in one and a variety ranging from cream to dark gray in others. You will also find some lovely picture rock at this site.

42. San Saba River Ranch Picnic Area

San Saba River site

See map on page 74.
Land type: Lightly forested hills, river plain
GPS: 31.003205 / -99.2682581
Elevation: 1,662 feet
Best time of year: Spring, early summer, late summer, fall. It may be snow covered in winter but otherwise OK.
Land manager: Texas Department of Transportation
Material: Flint
Tools: Geological hammer, short handle rake, garden shovel, spray bottle for the pieces lying around
Vehicle type: Good highway all the way. 2-wheel drive is sufficient.

San Saba material

Precautions and restrictions: Just be sure to not block the drive when parking. The area near the river can be slippery.

Accommodations: There are a number of motels in Katemcy and Brady. Brady is located near the geographical center of the Lone Star State. The Heart of Texas RV Park offers 20 full hookup back-in sites. The park boasts of good wildlife watching.

SPECIAL ATTRACTIONS

Enchanted Rock Natural Area is a must-see if you are in the area. It takes about an hour to drive there from Brady.

The massive pink granite dome rising above Central Texas has inspired many mystical legends about its ability to change people's lives. The rock has drawn people for thousands of years. The Natural Area is more than just the dome. The scenery, rock formations, and legends are magical, too. The area sports 11 miles of hiking trails, and rock climbing is a popular pastime here.

Another place of interest is the Texas Long Horn Caverns. This Texas state park was developed by the Civilian Conservation Corps. The park features an amazing cavern created by an ancient river—the caverns were discovered by

Anglo settlers in the 1870s. Visitors can choose from a number of different tours.

FINDING THE SITE

This picnic area is about 126 miles from Austin with a drive time of about 2 hours and 15 minutes. It is about 135 miles from San Antonio and it takes about 2 hours and 15 minutes to drive there. From Katemcy at the intersection of US 87 and Texas Farm Road 1222 drive 7 miles north on US 87 to the picnic area.

ROCKHOUNDING

There isn't too much material here, but we included it because of the wonderful wall that runs the distance of the perimeter of the rest area. The entire structure is made of concrete in which a lot of beautiful agates and fossils are imbedded. Many rock hounds would be interested in seeing this structure. There is a relatively easily hiked path down to the river. You can wander around the bank and pick up some small flint and agate pieces.

43. Brady Marine Fossils

Brady Fossil site

See map on page 74.
Land type: Lots of various vegetation including oak, cedar, and mesquite woodlands. These are interspersed with grass prairies.
GPS: 31.099985 / -99.3293417
Elevation: 1,759 feet
Best time of year: Spring, early summer, late summer, fall. It may be snow covered in winter but otherwise OK. Midsummer is also OK, but it can be very hot.
Land manager: Texas Department of Transportation
Material: Marine fossils
Tools: Geological hammer, short handle rake, garden shovel, spray bottle for the pieces lying around
Vehicle type: Good highway. 2-wheel drive is sufficient.
Precautions and restrictions: Parking can be tight. Pull well off the pavement. If you cannot pull off the pavement, drive on until you can and walk back. Use your warning flashers.

Brady Fossil site

Typical fossil found here

Accommodations: Rocking R RV Park is right in downtown Brady. They are dog friendly. They built a huge yard or dog run so your animals can run around for some exercise. This facility is a working ranch and raises a big variety of undulates. They have some wonderful longhorn cattle as well as domesticated deer.

SPECIAL ATTRACTIONS

If you are a country music fan, the Heart of Texas Country Music Museum is a must-see in Brady. Over one hundred artists are represented in the museum with stage costumes, musical instruments, autographs, posters and other memorabilia highlighting country music's colorful past. Of special interest to various collectors are pieces designed by some of the greatest tailors in the business including Nudie, Harvey Krantz, and Nathan Turk, among others.

Fine fishing can be had at the Brady Creek Reservoir. This lake is on Brady Creek in McCulloch County. The lake is just west of downtown Brady. The dam and lake are managed by the City of Brady. The reservoir was officially impounded in 1963.

FINDING THE SITE

Brady is about 128 miles northwest of Austin and is a 2-hour-and-20-minute drive. At the junction of US 87 and TX 71 at the south end of Brady, travel north on US 87 for 0.1 mile to the city limit sign. Then drive 0.3 mile farther to the site. You will find a road cut here consisting of light tan caliche rock.

ROCKHOUNDING

These are Pennsylvanian marine fossils. We found gastropods and crinoids. In addition, there is quite a bit of jasper, agate, and rhyolite lying around.

44. TX 71 Marine Fossils

Looking at the road cut from across the road

See map on page 74.

Land type: Lightly wooded and ranch land

GPS: 31.0099817 / -99.2072717

Elevation: 1,633 feet

Best time of year: Spring, early summer, late summer, fall. It may be snow covered in winter but otherwise OK. Midsummer is also OK, but it can be very hot.

Land manager: Texas Department of Transportation

Material: Marine fossils

Tools: Geological hammer, short handle rake, garden shovel, spray bottle

Vehicle type: Good road all the way. 2-wheel drive is sufficient.

Precautions and restrictions: Parking can be tight. Pull well off the pavement. If you cannot pull off the pavement, drive on until you can and walk back. Use your warning flashers.

Accommodations: Rocking R RV Park is right in downtown Brady. They are dog friendly and built a huge yard or dog run so your animals can run around for some

Typical fossil rock from this site

exercise. This facility is a working ranch and raises a big variety of undulates. They have some wonderful longhorn cattle as well as domesticated deer.

SPECIAL ATTRACTIONS

If you are a country music fan, the Heart of Texas Country Music Museum is a must-see in Brady. Over one hundred artists are represented in the museum with stage costumes, musical instruments, autographs, posters, and other memorabilia highlighting country music's colorful past. Of special interest to various collectors are pieces designed by some of the greatest tailors in the business including Nudie, Harvey Krantz, and Nathan Turk, among others.

Fine fishing can be had in the Brady Creek Reservoir. This lake is on Brady Creek in McCulloch County. The lake is just west of downtown Brady. The dam and lake are managed by the City of Brady. The reservoir was officially impounded in 1963.

FINDING THE SITE

This site is about 115 miles northwest of Austin and it takes about 2 hours to drive the distance. From the junction of US 87 and TX 71 at the southern end

The site

of the town of Brady, drive southeast on TX 71 for 9.5 miles to a large road cut on both sides of the road.

ROCKHOUNDING

We found marine fossils that included but were not limited to bivalves, a crinoid impression, and a striped rhyolite. Do not limit yourselves to this exact location This material can be found at almost every place you stop within a few miles of our GPS numbers.

45. Fly Gap Road Crystals

Fly Gap Road is usually well graded.

See map on page 74.

Land type: Lightly wooded, ranch land

GPS: Site A: 30.841675 / -99.054786; Site B: 30.8419631 / -99.0548448

Elevation: 1,612 feet for the first set of GPS numbers and 1,627 feet for the second

Best time of year: Spring, early summer, late summer, fall. It may be snow covered in winter but otherwise OK. Midsummer is also OK, but it can be very hot.

Land manager: Mason County Road Administration

Material: Quartz crystals

Tools: Geological hammer, short handle rake, garden shovel, spray bottle, full-size pick, gads, crowbar, sledgehammer, full-size shovel

Vehicle type: Well graded gravel road. It can get sloppy during inclement weather. 2-wheel drive is sufficient during good weather, otherwise 4-wheel drive is recommended.

Precautions and restrictions: Pulling off to the side of the road can be problematic. The grading leaves large berms. Be very careful when stopping. Though the traffic is very light, some vehicles do pass through. Another thing to be careful about is trespassing. The fence lines are missing from some sections of the road. These folks take trespassing very seriously. There have been incidents where rock hounds have been taken into custody by the sheriff. Though we don't know of any prosecutions, your day can be ruined by sitting in the sheriff's office for an afternoon.

Accommodations: Llano City Park has full hookups, pull-through sites, and back-in sites. It has all the amenities, and at the time of this writing was very reasonable. It includes 30- or 50-amp service, water and sewer hookups, picnic tables, showers, laundry, and Wi-Fi. This is a lovely spot overlooking the river where one can walk and possibly find pieces of llanite or other granites as well as flint, jasper, and agates. Llano also has Badu Park and Grenwelge Park, which are run by the county. Badu Park also offers RV campsites.

SPECIAL ATTRACTIONS

Enchanted Rock Natural Area is a must-see if you are in the area. It sits about 25 miles north-northeast of Llano. It takes about a half an hour to drive the distance.

The massive pink granite dome rising above Central Texas has inspired many mystical legends about its ability to change people's lives. The rock has drawn people for thousands of years. The Natural Area is more than just the dome. The scenery, rock formations, and legends are magical, too. The area sports 11 miles of hiking trails, and rock climbing is a popular pastime here.

FINDING THE SITE

Fly Gap Road is about 105 miles northwest from Austin. It takes about 2 hours to drive the distance. If you are coming from the north at the junction of TX 71 with Oak Street in the small town of Fredonia, drive south on TX 71 for 5.9 miles. Make a right (south) onto Fly Gap Road.

If you are approaching from the south in the town of Mason from the junction of US 87 and TX 29, drive 9.3 miles east on TX 29. Turn north onto Texas Farm Road 1900 and travel 7.7 miles and you will reach the junction of Texas Farm Road 2618 and Fly Gap Road. Turn right (north) onto Fly Gap Road.

Smoky quartz crystals embedded in granite

ROCKHOUNDING

This is a famous location for finding quartz crystals both clear and smoky. If it is sunny, you will notice lots of sparkling stones in the road. These are mostly pieces of quartz. We did not find any complete crystals in the road. However, there was evidence of folks digging in the ground and chiseling big boulders. The first set of GPS numbers is for a place we saw diggings. The second is for the western end of Fly Gap Road where the pavement begins near the junction of Texas Farm Roads 1900 and 2618.

46. Kerrville Flint and Agate

Land type: Lots of various vegetation including oak, cedar, and mesquite woodlands. These are interspersed with grass prairies.
GPS: 30.1296117 / -99.0669983
Elevation: 2,030 feet
Best time of year: Spring, early summer, late summer, fall. It may be snow covered in winter but otherwise OK. Midsummer is also OK, but it can be very hot.
Land manager: Texas Department of Transportation
Material: Flint, agate
Tools: Geological hammer, short handle rake, garden shovel, spray bottle
Vehicle type: Good road all the way. 2-wheel drive is sufficient.
Precautions and restrictions: Parking can be tight. Pull well off the pavement. If you cannot pull off the pavement, drive on until you can and walk back. Use your warning flashers.
Accommodations: The Kerrville-Schreiner Park along the Guadalupe River continues to be the city's busiest park. This city park offers a variety of fun camping options such as 30 -and 50-amp RV sites, tent camping, cabins, and even a Ranch House. Facilities include the recreation hall, dining hall, and day-use facilities including playground, butterfly garden, sand volleyball, basketball, 10-plus miles of hiking and biking trails, river access, River Trail Trailhead, kayak and canoe rentals, fishing, and picnic areas with standing grills throughout. With 517 acres, this is the largest municipal park in Kerrville. Buckhorn Lake Resort is an upscale RV resort. Full hookup sites start at about $50 per day or $300 per week. This place has all the bells and whistles to make your stay luxurious. Besides the above, there are a number of other RV resorts and campgrounds. The city also boasts a number of fine motels and other accommodations.

SPECIAL ATTRACTIONS

Five miles southeast of Kerrville one finds the Kerrville-Schreiner Park. It is a 517.2-acre area along the Guadalupe River, originally built by the CCC, the Civilian Conservation Corps, in the early 1930s. This park was formerly operated as a state park but the City of Kerrville now runs the property.

The Texas bluebonnet is one of the most plentiful and colorful of the native plants in the park. But the area offers a representative sampling of the

Sites 46–49

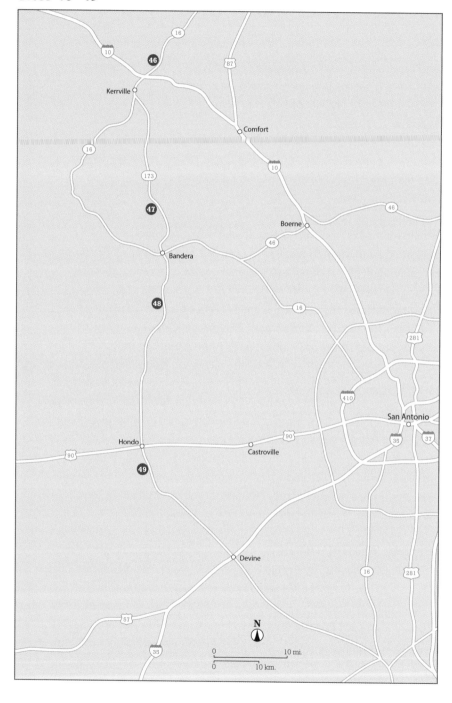

Kerrville chalcedony location

Hill Country landscape. There are acres of live oak, Spanish oak, and junipers populating the hills and arroyos. Other plants include redbud, sumac, buckeye, pecan, mesquite, and several other varieties of flowers.

White-tailed deer, which have made the Hill Country famous as a hunting area, abound in the park. Wildlife and bird watching are a favorite activity as the park bustles with squirrels, armadillos, turkeys, jackrabbits, mallard ducks, and several species of birds.

A variety of chalcedony is available here.

Good fishing can be accessed in the Guadalupe River. This water holds substantial populations of crappie, perch, catfish, and bass.

FINDING THE SITE

Kerrville is about a hundred miles west of Austin and it takes about 2 hours to drive the distance. This city is about 65 miles from San Antonio with the drive time of about an hour. From the junction of I-10 and TX 16, go north on TX 16 for 5 miles to a rocky road cut.

ROCKHOUNDING

The flint at this site is a nondescript gray. Some is mixed with a chocolate-colored chalcedony making them very attractive. Also found is a material with a blueish tint. A lot of these stones have to be chipped as it is difficult to determine what is inside due to weathering. Some pieces contain a very sparkly druzy quartz. When cleaned, they make for very interesting specimens.

47. Bandera Marine Fossils

See map on page 122.
Land type: Lots of various vegetation including oak, cedar, and mesquite woodlands. These are interspersed with grass prairies.
GPS: 29.91789 / -99.1112033
Elevation: 1,863 feet
Best time of year: Spring, early summer, late summer, fall. It may be snow covered in winter but otherwise OK. Midsummer is also OK, but it can be very hot.
Land manager: Texas Department of Transportation
Material: Marine fossils of the Glen Rose Formation
Tools: Geological hammer, garden shovel, short handle rake, spray bottle
Vehicle type: Good highway all the way. 2-wheel drive is sufficient.
Precautions and restrictions: Parking can be tight. Pull well off the pavement. If you cannot pull off the pavement, drive on until you can and walk back. Use your warning flashers.

The road containing fossils

Accommodations: The Hill Country State Natural Area offers walk-in and hike-in campsites. There are a total of about 20 sites, and each can accommodate between 4 and 8 people. Reservations are recommended. The natural area also has a lodge that sleeps 9 with a kitchen and bathroom. There are a number of commercial RV parks in Bandera as well as motels and other facilities.

SPECIAL ATTRACTIONS

Bandera claims to be the Cowboy Capital of the World. There are many dude ranches in the area. This is the central location of one of Texas's most scenic drives.

The Hill Country State Natural Area is a genuine back-to-nature experience. It covers more than 5,000 acres of rugged canyons, scenic plateaus, and tranquil creek bottoms. Hiking is the premier activity here along with horseback riding. The trails range from an easy 1-mile ramble to a rigorous backpacking trek through some real wilderness.

Guides are available for hire for the less experienced and adventuresome.

A must-see for all rock hounds and fossil collectors is the Bandera Natural History Museum. It is a large museum featuring natural history exhibits,

Abundant fossils in the rocks here

dinosaur and Ice Age mammal replicas, dioramas, and educational stations. They also have many local stones on display. They have over a hundred full-body animal mounts. The museum also has displays about the human history of the area.

FINDING THE SITE

Bandera is about 50 miles northwest of San Antonio and it takes about an hour to drive there. It is about 120 miles from Austin with a 2-hour drive time. From TX 173 and TX 16, drive north on TX 173 for 14.7 miles. You will see a very large road cut that continues for about a mile.

ROCKHOUNDING

You will find some very well preserved Lower Cretaceous marine fossils. The mix consists of, but is not limited to, bivalves including oysters, gastropods, crinoids, and Turritella snail shells.

The fossils found are of the Glen Rose Formation, which is yellowish as opposed to the grayish Edwards limestone in which other fossils are found. Search in the bottom of the road cut for the best finds.

48. Bandera Chocolate Agate

See map on page 122.

Land type: Lots of various vegetation including oak, cedar, and mesquite woodlands. These are interspersed with grass prairies.

GPS: 29.5165698 / -99.1083451

Elevation: 1,314 feet

Best time of year: Spring, early summer, late summer, fall. It may be snow covered in winter but otherwise OK. Midsummer is also OK, but it can be very hot.

Land manager: Texas Department of Transportation

Material: Agate, flint

Tools: Geological hammer, garden shovel, short handle rake, spray bottle. If you decide to make a go at extracting pieces from the wall, it would be necessary to be skilled in the use of gads, chisels, crowbars, and sledgehammers. Of course, you will also have to use some of your upper body muscles during the process.

Vehicle type: Good highway all the way. 2-wheel drive is sufficient.

Precautions and restrictions: Parking can be tight. Pull well off the pavement. If you cannot pull off the pavement, drive on until you can and walk back. Use your warning flashers.

Accommodations: The Hill Country State Natural Area offers walk-in and hike-in campsites. There are a total of about 20 sites, and each can accommodate between 4 and 8 people. Reservations are recommended. The natural area also has a lodge that sleeps 9 with a kitchen and bathroom. There are a number of commercial RV parks in Bandera as well as motels and other facilities.

SPECIAL ATTRACTIONS

Bandera claims to be the Cowboy Capital of the World. There are many dude ranches in the area. This is the central location of some of Texas's most scenic drives.

The Hill Country State Natural Area is a genuine back-to-nature experience. It covers more than 5,000 acres of rugged canyons, scenic plateaus, and tranquil creek bottoms. Hiking is the premier activity here along with horseback riding. The trails range from an easy 1-mile ramble to a rigorous backpacking trek through some real wilderness.

Guides are available for hire for the less experienced and adventuresome.

The pull-off is here.

A must-see for all rock hounds and fossil collectors is the Bandera Natural History Museum. It is a large museum featuring natural history exhibits, dinosaur and Ice Age mammal replicas, dioramas, and educational stations. They also have many local stones on display. They have over a hundred full-body animal mounts. The museum also has displays about the human history of the area.

Not just chocolate agate here

FINDING THE SITE

Bandera is about 50 miles northwest of San Antonio and it takes about an hour to drive there. It's about 120 miles from Austin with a 2-hour drive time. In Bandera from the junction of TX 16 and TX 173, travel TX 173 south for 15.8 miles to a large road cut.

If you are approaching from the south, in the town of Hondo, at the junction of US 90 and TX 173, travel 10 miles north on TX 173 to the road cut.

ROCKHOUNDING

This a massive road cut, and collecting is on both sides. The agate and flint are primarily several shades of chocolate and caramel. The prize pieces have swirls of red and gold. Besides all the small pieces lying around, there are large chunks that are quite weathered on the outside. These have to be chipped to reveal the beautiful material inside. While there is plenty of agate lying around, to get the best of this site it would be necessary to work the nodules out of the road cut walls. You could possibly extract some chunks that weigh more than 10 pounds.

49. Hondo Chocolate Agate and Flint

See map on page 122.
Land type: Lots of various vegetation including oak, cedar, and mesquite woodlands. These are interspersed with grass prairies.
GPS: 29.26211 / -99.07155
Elevation: 859 feet
Best time of year: Spring and early summer, late summer and fall. It may be snow covered in winter but otherwise OK. Midsummer is also OK, but it can be very hot.
Land manager: Texas Department of Transportation
Material: Flint, agate
Tools: Geological hammer, garden shovel, short handle rake, spray bottle
Vehicle type: Good highway all the way. 2-wheel drive is sufficient.
Precautions and restrictions: Parking can be tight. Pull well off the pavement. If you cannot pull off the pavement, drive on until you can and walk back. Use your warning flashers.

Material is found on both sides of the road here.

Pleasing colors in some of the pieces

Accommodations: There are many commercial RV parks and campgrounds in and around Hondo. The Quiet Texas RV Parks is located in Hondo. It sports a quiet country atmosphere while still being close to restaurants, grocery stores, a post office, and a laundry facility. The landscaped lots are large, with shade trees and hundreds of species of songbirds. The park has a wind-powered generator that makes clean renewable energy for their guests to use.

SPECIAL ATTRACTIONS

Hondo Nature Trail is a 0.8-mile loop trail near Hondo. It takes about 20–30 minutes to complete and is considered an easy route. This trail is almost never too busy. It is a nice, calm walk through the natural environment of the area. Because winter may be inclement, the best times to visit this trail are February through November.

FINDING THE SITE

Hondo is a city in and the county seat of Medina County. It sits 40 miles west of San Antonio. It takes about 45 minutes to drive there. From Hondo at the junction of US 90 and TX 173, drive 6.2 miles south on TX 173. The hillside here is gray rock. This is the location of the GPS numbers.

ROCKHOUNDING

The chalcedony consists of a number of shades of chocolate brown—very pretty. In addition, there are a number of marine fossils. These include but are not limited to oysters and other bivalves. Also present is a single shelled critter similar to abalone.

SOUTH TEXAS

This section of Texas, as with most areas, has a great number of rockhounding possibilities. The primary materials here are agate, petrified wood, jasper, and flint. These are often quite colorful and make excellent jewelry or display pieces when polished.

Some of the agate is clear with myriad colors in swirls. The wood includes some small pieces of palm wood. These are often very colorful and well agatized, appropriate for cutting.

Roadside collecting here is excellent and very widespread. The area around Choke Canyon Reservoir used to be a favorite collecting site for rock hounds. However, it is now a state park and off limits. But, no, there is no need to despair because the roadside in proximity of the lake can be littered with material available for pick up.

The region around Zapata and Falcon Reservoir is much the same. As of this writing, it is OK to collect along the shoreline as long as one avoids Falcon Lake State Park. Again, many of the roadsides are covered with fine material.

Weather-wise, collecting is good all year. It can be extremely hot in the summer. So make sure you carry a lot of water and sunscreen. We enjoy the area in the winter as the temperatures are usually quite pleasant.

Extra caution should be taken during warm weather here as well as all throughout Texas. This area holds a particularly large population of reptiles. Always carry a snake stick and rattle, and brush with it before stepping close. There may be a very upset critter under your foot if you don't. Look a stone completely over before putting it the bag. You do not want any unwelcome hitchhikers.

50. Tilden Petrified Wood

Land type: Texas brush country; mesquite, cactus, small oaks, and bunch grass
GPS: Site A: 28.6686833 / -98.541447; Site B: 28.6286667 / -98.54646
Elevation: Site A: 455 feet; Site B: 392 feet
Best time of year: Late fall, winter, spring, early summer
Land manager: Texas Department of Transportation
Material: Petrified wood, flint, agate
Tools: Geological hammer, garden shovel, short handle rake, spray bottle
Vehicle type: Good highway all the way. 2-wheel drive is sufficient.
Precautions and restrictions: Parking can be tight. Pull well off the pavement. If you cannot pull off the pavement, drive on until you can and walk back. Use your warning flashers. Watch for snakes when the temperature is above 45°F.
Accommodations: Choke Canyon State Park offers over 100 campsites with electric and water and 9 walk-in tent sites. This is a lovely campground, and we have spent a lot of time here. In addition to the park, there are quite a few commercial RV resorts and campgrounds and fish camps in the area.

The pullout at the Tilden site

Sites 50–60

These pieces will make fine polished pieces.

SPECIAL ATTRACTIONS

Fishing in Choke Canyon Lake is excellent. Blue catfish can be targeted from the shore or boat. Very large flathead catfish roam the bottom of the lake. In the spring, white bass are the attraction, as are crappie. Some of catches are very sizable. And, of course, largemouth bass fishing is excellent.

The Longhorn Museum in Pleasanton is certainly worth a visit. The museum, through its displays of artifacts, documents, portraits, and written excerpts, portrays the history of Atascosa County. The museum devotes major efforts in documenting the area as the "Birthplace of the Cowboy."

FINDING THE SITE

Tilden is about 80 miles south of San Antonio and it takes about an hour and a half to drive there. To get to Site A, in Jourdanton at the intersection of TX 97 and TX 16, drive south on TX 16 for 17.4 miles.

To get to Site B continue on from Site A on TX 16 for another 2.8 miles.

ROCKHOUNDING

Both of these locations sport a lot of petrified wood along with an occasional rare piece of palm wood. We also found pretty flint and a few agates. At both of these sites there are a few pieces lying around, but to find the best, one must dig and then chip each suspected stone. Do not confine yourselves to the two sites we describe. Make a number of stops along TX 16. Most will yield good material.

51. Frio River Petrified Wood

See map on page 135.
Land type: Texas brush country; mesquite, cactus, small oaks, and bunch grass
GPS: 28.4678167 / -98.5477617
Elevation: 257 feet
Best time of year: Late fall, winter, spring, early summer
Land manager: Texas Department of Transportation
Material: Petrified wood, flint, agate
Tools: Geological hammer, garden shovel, short handle rake, spray bottle
Vehicle type: Good highway all the way. 2-wheel drive is sufficient.
Precautions and restrictions: Parking can be tight. Pull well off the pavement. If you cannot pull off the pavement, drive on until you can and walk back. Use your warning flashers. Watch for snakes when the temperature is above 45°F.
Accommodations: Choke Canyon State Park offers over 100 campsites with electric and water and 9 walk-in tent sites. This is a lovely campground, and we have spent a lot of time here. In addition to the park, there are quite a few commercial RV resorts and campgrounds and fish camps in the area.

The Frio River bridge

Typical chalcedony from the Frio River

SPECIAL ATTRACTIONS
Fishing in Choke Canyon Lake is excellent. Blue catfish can be targeted from the shore or boat. Very large flathead catfish roam the bottom of the lake. In the spring, white bass are the attraction, as are crappie. Some of the catches are very sizable. And, of course, largemouth bass fishing is excellent.

The Longhorn Museum in Pleasanton is certainly worth a visit. The museum, through its displays of artifacts, documents, portraits, and written excerpts, portrays the history of Atascosa County. The museum devotes major efforts in documenting the area as the "Birthplace of the Cowboy."

FINDING THE SITE
Tilden is about 80 miles from San Antonio and it takes about an hour and a half to drive there. There are two different junctions of TX 72 and TX 16. Find the one where TX 72 comes in from the west and meets TX 16. Drive south on TX 16 for 0.2 mile and park at the Frio River Bridge.

ROCKHOUNDING
Good collecting of petrified wood can be had along the banks of the Frio River. We could not get to the river from the bridge because the water was too high, but there are a lot reliable reports of good collecting here. A lot of this material is palm wood. In reality, it pays to check out almost any road in this region. Nearly all will hold some material.

52. TX 72 Petrified Wood and Agate

See map on page 135.

Land type: Texas brush country; mesquite, cactus, small oaks, and bunch grass

GPS: 28.4602133 / -98.47188

Elevation: 467 feet

Best time of year: Late fall, winter, spring, early summer

Land manager: Texas Department of Transportation

Material: Petrified wood, flint, agate

Tools: Geological hammer, garden shovel, short handle rake, spray bottle

Vehicle type: Good highway all the way. 2-wheel drive is sufficient.

Precautions and restrictions: Parking can be tight. Pull well off the pavement. If you cannot pull off the pavement, drive on until you can and walk back. Use your warning flashers. Watch for snakes when the temperature is above 45°F.

The location at TX 72

Interesting agates from TX 72

Accommodations: Choke Canyon State Park offers over 100 campsites with electric and water and 9 walk-in tent sites. This is a lovely campground, and we have spent a lot of time here. In addition to the park, there are quite a few commercial RV resorts and campgrounds and fish camps in the area.

SPECIAL ATTRACTIONS

Fishing in Choke Canyon Lake is excellent. Blue catfish can be targeted from the shore or boat. Very large flathead catfish roam the bottom of the lake. In the spring, white bass are the attraction, as are crappie. Some of the catches are very sizable. And, of course, largemouth bass fishing is excellent.

The Longhorn Museum in Pleasanton is certainly worth a visit. The museum, through its displays of artifacts, documents, portraits, and written excerpts, portrays the history of Atascosa County. The museum devotes major efforts in documenting the area as the "Birthplace of the Cowboy."

FINDING THE SITE

Tilden is about 80 miles from San Antonio and it takes about an hour and a half to drive there. From TX 16 and TX 72 in Tilden, drive east 4.6 miles on TX 72. There is a large area of erosion on the south side of the road. A hint: The palm wood is often hidden beneath very weathered surfaces. However, these are relatively easy to spot because they are usually black, gray, or a combination of both.

ROCKHOUNDING

In just a few minutes, we found a pocketful of tumblers and a few slicers. Do not limit yourselves to this site. There is a lot of material including quality palm wood and clear agates with colorful inclusions throughout this area and most of the way to Three Rivers. Stop often and check places out.

53. Texas Farm Road 99 Agate, Flint, and Petrified Wood

The pull-off on Texas Farm Road 99

See map on page 135.

Land type: Texas brush country; mesquite, cactus, small oaks, and bunch grass

GPS: 28.5039933 / -98.416685

Elevation: 365 feet

Best time of year: Late fall, winter, spring, early summer

Land manager: Texas Department of Transportation

Material: Petrified wood, flint, agate

Tools: Geological hammer, garden shovel, short handle rake, spray bottle

Vehicle type: Good highway all the way. 2-wheel drive is sufficient.

Precautions and restrictions: Parking can be tight. Pull well off the pavement. If you cannot pull off the pavement, drive on until you can walk back. Use your warning flashers. Watch for snakes when the temperature is above 45°F.

Accommodations: Choke Canyon State Park offers over 100 campsites with electric and water and 9 walk-in tent sites. This is a lovely campground, and we have spent a lot of time here. In addition to the park, there are quite a few commercial RV resorts and campgrounds and fish camps in the area.

Texas Farm Road 99 wood

SPECIAL ATTRACTIONS

Fishing in Choke Canyon Lake is excellent. Blue catfish can be targeted from the shore or boat. Very large flathead catfish roam the bottom of the lake. In the spring, white bass are the attraction, as are crappie. Some of the catches are very sizable. And, of course, largemouth bass fishing is excellent.

The Longhorn Museum in Pleasanton is certainly worth a visit. The museum, through its displays of artifacts, documents, portraits, and written excerpts, portrays the history of Atascosa County. The museum devotes major efforts in documenting the area as the "Birthplace of the Cowboy."

FINDING THE SITE

Tilden is about 80 miles from San Antonio and it takes about an hour and a half to drive there. From the junction of TX 72 and TX 16 in Tilden, drive east on TX 72 for 6.6 miles. Turn left (north) onto Texas Farm Road 99 for 3.5 miles to an eroded area on the west side (left).

ROCKHOUNDING

As we said previously, there is a lot of material in this area. We found a good quantity of agate, flint, jasper, and petrified wood here. Do not limit yourselves to this exact location. If you have time check out other areas between here and the bridge to the north.

54. Recreation Road 7 Flint and Jasper

See map on page 135.
Land type: Texas brush country; mesquite, cactus, small oaks, and bunch grass
GPS: 28460855 / -98.4183867
Elevation: 352 feet
Best time of year: Late fall, winter, spring, early summer
Land manager: Texas Department of Transportation
Material: Flint, jasper, petrified wood
Tools: Geological hammer, garden shovel, short handle rake, spray bottle
Vehicle type: Good highway all the way. 2-wheel drive is sufficient.
Precautions and restrictions: Parking can be tight. Pull well off the pavement. If you cannot pull off the pavement, drive on until you can and walk back. Use your warning flashers. Carry a snake stick and use it when the temperature is above 45°F. Be careful not to wander onto state park land where rockhounding is prohibited.

Recreation Road 7 site

Accommodations: Choke Canyon State Park offers over 100 campsites with electric and water and 9 walk-in tent sites. This is a lovely campground, and we have spent a lot of time here. In addition to the park, there are quite a few commercial RV resorts and campgrounds and fish camps in the area.

SPECIAL ATTRACTIONS

Fishing in Choke Canyon Lake is excellent. Blue catfish can be targeted from the shore or boat. Very large flat-head catfish roam the bottom of the lake. In the spring, white bass are the

Nice tumblers from Recreation Road 7

attraction, as are crappie. Some of the catches are very sizable. And, of course, largemouth bass fishing is excellent.

FINDING THE SITE

Tilden is about 80 miles from San Antonio and it takes about an hour and a half to drive there. From the junction of TX 72 and TX 16 in Tilden, drive east on TX 72 for 6.6 miles to Texas Farm Road 99. From the junction of TX 72 and Texas Farm Road 99 continue east on TX 72 for 1.2 miles. Turn left (northeast) onto Recreation Road 7. Drive 0.2 mile. That's where the GPS numbers were taken.

ROCKHOUNDING

We found a good quantity of agate, flint, jasper, and petrified wood here. Do not limit yourselves to this location. There is material almost at every stop.

55. Farm Road 437 Flint, Jasper, and Petrified Wood

See map on page 135.

Land type: Texas brush country; mesquite, cactus, small oaks, and bunch grass

GPS: 28.6481576 / -98.2426981

Elevation: 2,820 feet

Best time of year: Late fall, winter, spring, early summer

Land manager: Texas Department of Transportation

Material: Petrified wood, flint, jasper, agate

Tools: Geological hammer, garden shovel, short handle rake, spray bottle

Vehicle type: Good highway all the way. 2-wheel drive is sufficient.

Precautions and restrictions: Parking can be tight. Pull well off to the side of this gravel road. During our time here there was little traffic, but be sure you are leaving enough room for other vehicles to pass. Use your warning flashers. Watch for snakes and carry and use a snake stick when the temperature is above 45°F.

Accommodations: Choke Canyon State Park offers over 100 campsites with electric and water and 9 walk-in tent sites. This is a lovely campground, and we have spent a lot of time here. In addition to the park, there are quite a few commercial RV resorts and campgrounds and fish camps in the area.

The site at Farm Road 437

Material from Farm Road 437

SPECIAL ATTRACTIONS

The Longhorn Museum in Pleasanton is certainly worth a visit. The museum, through its displays of artifacts, documents, portraits, and written excerpts, portrays the history of Atascosa County. The museum devotes major efforts in documenting the area as the "Birthplace of the Cowboy."

FINDING THE SITE

Whitsett is an unincorporated community in northwestern Live Oak County. It is about 62 miles south of San Antonio with a drive time of about an hour. In Whitsett, from the junction of Texas Farm Road 99 and US 281, drive south 0.8 mile to Texas Farm Road 437. The road continues east for 1.8 miles and ends at the I-37 Southbound Rest Area. You can also drive to the Southbound Rest Area off I-37 just south of the exit to Whitsett. From here you can walk across the service road to the opposite end of Texas Farm Road 437.

ROCKHOUNDING

Sometimes serendipity plays a big part in the rockhounding experience. We were driving down I-37 toward Corpus Christi and the dog needed to be walked. We just happened to take her across the service road to Texas Farm Road 437, which is gravel. At once we noticed a number of pieces of flint and petrified wood. The GPS numbers are for the end of the road, but good pieces can be found along the entire 1.8-mile length of the road.

56. Whitsett Banded Limestone and Flint

See map on page 135.

Land type: Texas brush country; mesquite, cactus, small oaks, and bunch grass

GPS: 28.64668 / -98.2846283

Elevation: 338 feet

Best time of year: Late fall, winter, spring, early summer

Land manager: Texas Department of Transportation

Material: Banded limestone, flint

Tools: Geological hammer, garden shovel, short handle rake, spray bottle

Vehicle type: Good highway all the way. 2-wheel drive is sufficient.

Precautions and restrictions: Parking can be tight. Pull well off the pavement. If you cannot pull off the pavement, drive on until you can and walk back. Use your warning flashers. Watch for snakes, and carry and use a snake stick when the temperature is above 45°F.

Accommodations: Choke Canyon State Park offers over 100 campsites with electric and water and 9 walk-in tent sites. This is a lovely campground, and

Whitsettt Limestone site

Nice limestone and flint from Whitsett

we have spent a lot of time here. In addition to the park there are quite a few commercial RV resorts and campgrounds and fish camps in the area.

SPECIAL ATTRACTIONS

The Longhorn Museum in Pleasanton is certainly worth a visit. The museum, through its displays of artifacts, documents, portraits, and written excerpts, portrays the history of Atascosa County. The museum devotes major efforts in documenting the area as the "Birthplace of the Cowboy."

FINDING THE SITE

Whitsett is an unincorporated community in northwestern Live Oak County. It is about 62 miles south of San Antonio with a drive time of about an hour. From the junction of Texas Farm Road 99 and US 281 in Whitsett, drive north 1.8 miles on US 281. You will find a large mound of limestone on the east (right) side of the road.

ROCKHOUNDING

These piles look like they've been around for a while since there is grass growing on them. Dig around them and you will find some nice pieces of banded limestone. The colors range from white to dark gray and even to brown. Pick the ones with the most contrasted color bands. They polish up well. There also is a good quantity of flint from gray to brown in color.

57. Falls City Agate

See map on page 135.
Land type: Texas brush country; mesquite, cactus, small oaks, and bunch grass
GPS: 28.9751283 / -98.037175
Elevation: 127.3 feet
Best time of year: Late fall, winter, spring, early summer
Land manager: Texas Department of Transportation
Material: Jasper, flint, agates
Tools: Geological hammer, garden shovel, short handle rake, spray bottle
Vehicle type: Good highway all the way. 2-wheel drive is sufficient.
Precautions and restrictions: Parking can be tight. Pull well off the pavement. If you cannot pull off the pavement, drive on until you can and walk back. Use your warning flashers.

Falls City site

Accommodations: There are a few RV parks in Kenedy, which is about 15 miles south of Falls City. These are: Pecan Grove RV Park, Kenedy RV Park, and Brown's Corner RV Park. All offer a variety of camping experiences. Motels can be found at Karnes City about 25 miles south of Falls City and Kenedy, 15 miles south of Falls City. You're not very far from metropolitan San Antonio, which offers an abundance of hotels and motels.

SPECIAL ATTRACTIONS
The Longhorn Museum in Pleasanton is certainly worth a visit. The museum, through its displays of artifacts, documents, portraits, and written excerpts,

Agate and flint from Falls City

portrays the history of Atascosa County. The museum devotes major efforts in documenting the area as the "Birthplace of the Cowboy."

FINDING THE SITE

Falls City is a city in Karnes County. It is about 45 miles southeast of San Antonio and takes about an hour to drive there. Drive southwest on Texas Farm Road 791 from Falls City; at the junction of Texas Farm Road 887, the site is on the south (left) side of the road.

ROCKHOUNDING

This area is great for rockhounding. Do not confine yourselves to this site alone. Make frequent stops where pulling off is easy. Check sites in both directions of Falls City. The origin of this material is most likely from the Lower Tertiary Era. It was formed in nodules and veins within a limestone bed. The softer limestone eventually eroded away leaving the chalcedony.

The petrified wood is quite colorful and very well agatized. Also keep an eye out for the pure white agate. Folks looking for tumblers will not be disappointed. Searching with due diligence will produce larger pieces up to grapefruit size. The pieces are mostly float, but digging may reveal some larger specimens.

58. Campbellton Marine Fossils

See map on page 135.

Land type: Texas brush country; mesquite, cactus, small oaks, and bunch grass

GPS: 28.69254 / -98.2921217

Elevation: 319 feet

Best time of year: Late fall, winter, spring, early summer

Land manager: Texas Department of Transportation

Material: Marine fossils

Tools: Geological hammer, garden shovel, short handle rake, spray bottle

Vehicle type: Good highway all the way. 2-wheel drive is sufficient.

Precautions and restrictions: Parking can be tight. Pull well off the pavement. If you cannot pull off the pavement, drive on until you can and walk back. Use your warning flashers.

Accommodations: Choke Canyon State Park offers over 100 campsites with electric and water and 9 walk-in tent sites. This is a lovely campground, and we have spent a lot of time here. In addition to the park, there are quite a few commercial RV resorts and campgrounds and fish camps in the area.

Pull-off at the Campbellton Fossil site

A limb cast from Campbellton

SPECIAL ATTRACTIONS
The Longhorn Museum in Pleasanton is certainly worth a visit. The museum, through its displays of artifacts, documents, portraits, and written excerpts, portrays the history of Atascosa County. The museum devotes major efforts in documenting the area as the "Birthplace of the Cowboy."

FINDING THE SITE
From the junction of Texas Farm Road 791 and US 281 drive south 4 miles on US 281. There are areas of erosion on both sides of the road.

ROCKHOUNDING
There are some very good specimens of crinoids and clams at this location. They are from the Pennsylvanian Era. If you don't see what you like on the surface, scrape around a bit with your geological hammer. Keep your eyes open for the petrified wood that is also present. These are mostly small pieces, but there are large ones present also. Some are quite colorful.

59. Whitsett Selenite

The large white area is very prominent.

See map on page 135.
Land type: Texas brush country; mesquite, cactus, small oaks, and bunch grass
GPS: 28.5893867 / -98.2124283
Elevation: 260 feet
Best time of year: Late fall, winter, spring, early summer
Land manager: Texas Department of Transportation
Material: Selenite
Tools: Geological hammer, garden shovel, short handle rake, and spray bottle for small pieces. If you want a bigger chunk for carving, sledgehammer, gads, chisels, pry bars, goggles, heavy duty gloves, and lots of muscle are required.
Vehicle type: Good highway all the way. 2-wheel drive is sufficient.

Precautions and restrictions: Parking can be tight. Pull well off to the side of this gravel road. During our time here there was little traffic but be sure you are leaving enough room for other vehicles to pass. Use your warning flashers. Watch for snakes and carry a snake stick and use it when the temperature is above 45°F. Use all the safety equipment suggested.

Accommodations: Choke Canyon State Park offers over 100 campsites with electric and water and 9 walk-in tent sites. This is a lovely campground, and we have spent a lot of time here. In addition to the park, there are quite a few commercial RV resorts and campgrounds and fish camps in the area.

SPECIAL ATTRACTIONS

The Longhorn Museum in Pleasanton is certainly worth a visit. The museum, through its displays of artifacts, documents, portraits, and written excerpts, portrays the history of Atascosa County. The museum devotes major efforts in documenting the area as the "Birthplace of the Cowboy."

FINDING THE SITE

Whitsett is an unincorporated community in northwestern Live Oak County. It is about 62 miles south of San Antonio with a drive time of about an hour. In Campbellton at the junction of Texas Farm Road 791 and US 281, travel south on US 281 for 13.4 miles.

ROCKHOUNDING

This was another serendipitous find for us. We were looking for a selenite outcropping in Campbellton that is no longer there. Perhaps the road had been rerouted over the decades. After giving up and heading toward the next location, we passed a large outcropping of white material. Turning the camper around, we quickly figured out that this was the material we were looking for only about 10 miles from the area described. There were small pieces below the outcropping suitable for small carvings. For larger pieces, one will have to chisel out a chunk.

60. Three Rivers Agate

See map on page 135.
Land type: South Texas brush country; mesquite, cactus, small oaks, and bunch grass
GPS: 28.42547 / -98.170865
Elevation: 227 feet
Best time of year: Late fall, winter, spring, early summer
Land manager: Texas Department of Transportation
Material: Agate, jasper, petrified wood, flint
Tools: Geological hammer, garden shovel, short handle rake, spray bottle
Vehicle type: Good highway all the way. 2-wheel drive is sufficient.

The Three River Agate site

Precautions and restrictions: There is a warning sign about a natural gas pipeline. Don't dig too deep. This is a narrow road. Pull-offs are scarce. The GPS numbers are at the one we found. Parking can be tight. This road is gravel and narrow. There was little traffic during our time there, but make sure you pull well off the middle of the road. If you cannot pull off to the side, drive on until you can and walk back. Use your warning flashers. Watch for snakes, and carry and use snake sticks when the temperature is above 45°F.

Accommodations: Choke Canyon State Park offers over 100 campsites with electric and water and 9 walk-in tent sites. This is a lovely campground, and we have spent a lot of time here. In addition to the park, there are quite a few commercial RV resorts and campgrounds and fish camps in the area.

Nice assortment of tumblers from Three Rivers

SPECIAL ATTRACTIONS

The Longhorn Museum in Pleasanton is certainly worth a visit. The museum, through its displays of artifacts, documents, portraits, and written excerpts, portrays the history of Atascosa County. The museum devotes major efforts in documenting the area as the "Birthplace of the Cowboy."

FINDING THE SITE

In the town of Three Rivers from the junction of TX 72 and US 281 drive 2.5 miles south on US 281. After crossing the Nueces River Bridge, turn east (left) onto Texas Farm Road 301. Drive 0.4 mile to the exposed area on both sides of the road. Be aware that when we were there Google Maps named the road as Texas Farm Road 313, but the sign on the road called it Texas Farm Road 301.

ROCKHOUNDING

There is a great variety of material here, but most of it is small. We found petrified wood of numerous colors, flint, and jasper in many shades. Also present are clear agates that resemble chalcedony roses. Do not confine yourselves to this stop. Nice pieces can be found all along this dead-end road.

61. San Diego Limestone

Land type: South Texas brush country; mesquite, cactus, small oaks, and bunch grass; ranch land of rolling hills and thick brush
GPS: 27.6423689 / -98.3516482
Elevation: 388 feet
Best time of year: Late fall, winter, spring, early summer
Land manager: Texas Department of Transportation
Material: Limestone
Tools: Geological hammer, garden shovel, short handle rake, spray bottle
Vehicle type: Good highway all the way. 2-wheel drive is sufficient.
Precautions and restrictions: Parking can be tight. Pull well off the pavement. If you cannot pull off the pavement, drive on until you can and walk back. Use your warning flashers. Watch for snakes, and carry and use a snake stick when the temperature is above 45°F.
Accommodations: There are a number of private campgrounds and motels in Freer.

Look around poles where erosion has occurred.

Sites 61–62, 68–70

Interesting multicolor limestone

SPECIAL ATTRACTIONS
Freer County Park offers a picnic area.

FINDING THE SITE
San Diego is a city in Duval and Jim Wells Counties. It is about 50 miles west of Corpus Christi and an hour's drive. In the town of San Diego from the junction of TX 44 and TX 359, turn south on TX 359 and travel 11 miles. You will see an eroded area on the west side around a telephone pole.

ROCKHOUNDING
Some of the limestone here is salmon colored but most is white or gray. The salmon color is very faint but is enhanced upon taking a polish and is very handsome. Some of this appears to be dendritic. Dendrites occur when manganese permeates the rock and forms interesting black patterns. They make for very attractive finished pieces.

Do not confine yourselves to the one location. These deposits extend for many miles along this road.

62. South of Freer Agate and Petrified Wood

See map on page 159.

Land type: South Texas brush country; mesquite, cactus, small oaks, and bunch grass; ranch land of rolling hills and thick brush

GPS: 27.582595 / -98.6556183

Elevation: 609 feet

Best time of year: Late fall, winter, spring, early summer

Land manager: Texas Department of Transportation

Material: Agate, petrified wood, jasper, flint

Tools: Geological hammer, garden shovel, short handle rake, spray bottle

Vehicle type: Good highway all the way. 2-wheel drive is sufficient.

Precautions and restrictions: Parking can be tight. Pull well off the pavement. If you cannot pull off the pavement, drive on until you can and walk back. Use your warning flashers. Watch for snakes, and carry and use a snake stick when the temperature is above 45°F.

Find interesting material within a few hundred yards of this area.

Very interesting material here

Accommodations: There are a number of private campgrounds and motels in Freer.

SPECIAL ATTRACTIONS
Freer County Park offers a picnic area.

Finding the Site

Freer is a city in Duval County and is 81 miles west of Corpus Christi, and it takes about an hour and a half to drive there. From San Diego at the junction of TX 44 and TX 359, turn south onto TX 359 for 16.5 miles to the town of Benavides. Turn west on Texas Farm Road 2295 for 14.8 miles to its junction with TX 16. Turn north on TX 16 for 0.4 mile to a large road cut.

ROCKHOUNDING
This was quite a stop. The agates here are really unique. The color range is really wide. The most unusual agates are a dark translucent with swirls of red running through them. The white banded agate is also very attractive. Some of the agates are clear with gold and brown round inclusions. Also found were nice pieces of petrified wood along with some palm wood. There also is a good variety of jasper in this road cut. Unlike many other locations, it appears that the good collecting was only at this road cut. We stopped at others without success.

63. Falcon Heights Agate and Petrified Wood

Land type: South Texas brush country; mesquite, cactus, small oaks, and bunch grass
GPS: 26.578512 / -99.128749
Elevation: 447 feet
Best time of year: Late fall, winter, spring, early summer
Land manager: Texas Department of Transportation
Material: Many varieties of chalcedony: agate, jasper, petrified wood, flint
Tools: Geological hammer, small shovel, spray bottle, short handle rake
Vehicle type: Good highway all the way. 2-wheel drive is sufficient.
Precautions and restrictions: Be careful to not wander into the state park. It is illegal to collect rocks there. Pull your vehicle well off the road and use your flashers. Please fill in and stamp down any holes you dig. Snakes are active when the temperature is higher than 45°F. Carry and use a snake stick.

Park well off the road here.

Sites 63–67

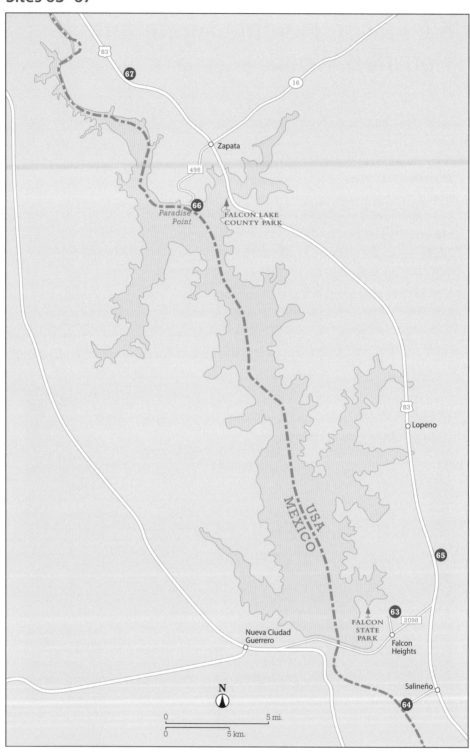

83

67

16

Zapata

496

66

Paradise
Point

FALCON LAKE
COUNTY PARK

83

Lopeno

USA
MEXICO

65

FALCON
STATE
PARK

63

2098

Nueva Ciudad
Guerrero

Falcon
Heights

N

Salineño

64

0   5 mi.

0   5 km.

Accommodations: Nice camping at Falcon Lake State Park or Falcon City Park. The sites range from full hookups to water-only tenting and small RV sites. There also are quite a few commercial RV parks and campgrounds in the area. Also there are hotels and motels in Zapata and Roma.

SPECIAL ATTRACTIONS

Excellent fishing is in Falcon Lake. There are a number of bass tournaments on the lake every year. Eight- to 10-pound fish are relatively common. Fishing for catfish is excellent. A boat is usually needed during the day, but catfish can be caught from the bank in the early morning and evening. Sunfish are abundant and not only a great attraction for children but can also make for a great dinner.

The animal sanctuary at Salineño offers great opportunities to observe birds, butterflies, and other wildlife.

The Zapata County Museum of History is very entertaining and educational.

On the Mexican side of the border, the ruins of the original house of Emiliano Zapata can be visited. He was one of Mexico's most iconic

A nice mix of material here

revolutionaries. It has been set up as museum in the village of Cuautla in the municipality of Ayala.

FINDING THE SITE

From the junction of US 83 and Texas Farm Road 2098, drive west for 2.6 miles on Texas Farm Road 2098. Turn north onto Falcon State Park Road and travel 0.9 mile. The site is on the west (left) just before the entrance to the park.

ROCKHOUNDING

This site is the location of a large gravelly area. There is a large variety of material here. Agate and jasper are quite common, but some pretty petrified wood and jasper can also be found. There are a lot of tumblers, but some larger slicers are also present. Again, do not confine yourselves to this exact location. Almost anywhere you stop, material will be found. In fact, even along Texas Farm Road 2098 many stops could be worthwhile.

64. Salineño Agate and Petrified Wood

See map on page 164.

Land type: South Texas brush country; mesquite, cactus, small oaks, and bunch grass; brushy river front

GPS: 26.5150882 / -99.1155446

Elevation: 227 feet

Best time of year: Late fall, winter, spring, early summer

Land manager: Texas Department of Transportation

Material: Petrified wood, agate, flint, jasper

Tools: Geological hammer, garden shovel, short handle rake, spray bottle

Vehicle type: Good highway all the way. 2-wheel drive is sufficient, but the last 0.2 mile is gravel and narrow and can be rather bumpy.

Precautions and restrictions: The area is quite brushy so be aware that there might be some snakes about. Make sure you know where you are stepping. Carry

Plenty can be found here by just walking around.

Nice material here

and use a snake stick when near brush. When picking up a stone, always check the bottom. There may be some insect or arachnid attached. Parking can be tight. There is a small parking area and a rough boat ramp at the end. Pull well off to the side and make sure to leave room for anyone attempting to put their boat in the river.

Accommodations: Nice camping at Falcon Lake State Park or Falcon City Park. The sites range from full hookups to water-only tenting and small RV sites. There also are quite a few commercial RV parks and campgrounds in the area. Also there are hotels and motels in Zapata and Roma.

SPECIAL ATTRACTIONS

Excellent fishing is in Falcon Lake. There are a number of bass tournaments on the lake every year. Eight- to 10-pound fish are relatively common. Fishing for catfish is excellent. A boat is usually needed during the day, but catfish can be caught from the bank in the early morning and evening. Sunfish are abundant and not only a great attraction for children but can also make for a great dinner.

The animal sanctuary at Salineño offers great opportunities to observe birds, butterflies, and other wildlife.

The Zapata County Museum of History is very entertaining and educational.

On the Mexican side of the border, the ruins of the original house of Emiliano Zapata can be visited. He was one of Mexico's most iconic revolutionaries. It has been set up as a museum in the village of Cuautla in the municipality of Ayala.

FINDING THE SITE

Zapata is a city in Zapata County along the Rio Grande. It is about 200 miles south of San Antonio, and it takes about three and a half hours to drive there. Falcon Heights is about 30 miles south of Zapata with a 35-minute drive time. From the town of Falcon Heights at the junction of US 83 and Texas Farm Road 2098, drive south on US 83 for 4.1 miles. At the junction with Salineño Road, turn west (right) and drive 1.7 miles eventually through the town of Salineño. At this point the hard top ends and the road narrows. Continue 0.2 mile to an open area on the banks of the Rio Grande River.

ROCKHOUNDING

If there are rock hounds' paradises, this place is surely one of them. There is a great variety of chalcedony both as large and small stones. Some very colorful petrified wood is also present including palm wood. The prize here is the dark agate with all different shaped red inclusions. You will also find some fossilized agatized shells. One of the great benefits of this site is that it is on the Rio Grande River so you can wash your finds and see what you have.

65. US 83 Agate and Petrified Wood

See map on page 164.
Land type: South Texas brush country; mesquite, cactus, small oaks, and bunch grass; open land, rolling hills with scrub
GPS: 26.6771 / -99.1067924
Elevation: 457 feet
Best time of year: Late fall, winter, spring, early summer
Land manager: Texas Department of Transportation
Material: Agate, jasper, petrified wood, flint
Tools: Geological hammer, garden shovel, short handle rake, spray bottle
Vehicle type: Good highway all the way. 2-wheel drive is sufficient.
Precautions and restrictions: Parking can be tight. Pull well off the pavement. If you cannot pull off the pavement, drive on until you can and walk back. Use your warning flashers. Watch for snakes, and carry and use a snake stick when the temperature is above 45°F.

Image of the site

Accommodations: Nice camping at Falcon Lake State Park or Falcon City Park. The sites range from full hookups to water-only tenting and small RV sites. There also are quite a few commercial RV parks and campgrounds in area. Also there are hotels and motels in Zapata and Roma.

SPECIAL ATTRACTIONS

Excellent fishing is in Falcon Lake. There are a number of bass tournaments on the lake every year. Eight- to 10-pound fish are relatively common. Fishing for catfish is excellent. A boat is usually needed during the day, but catfish can be caught from the bank in the early morning and evening. Sunfish are abundant and not only a great attraction for children but can also make for a great dinner.

The animal sanctuary at Salineño offers great opportunities to observe birds, butterflies, and other wildlife.

The Zapata County Museum of History is very entertaining and educational.

On the Mexican side of the border, the ruins of the original house of Emiliano Zapata can be visited. He was one of Mexico's most iconic revolutionaries. It has been set up as museum in the village of Cuautla in the municipality of Ayala.

Plenty of petrified wood here

FINDING THE SITE

Zapata is a city in Zapata County along the Rio Grande. It is about 200 miles south of San Antonio and it takes about three and a half hours to drive there. Falcon Heights is about 30 miles south of Zapata with a 35-minute drive time. From Falcon Heights at the junction of US 83 and Texas Farm Road 2098, drive 6.4 miles north on US 83 to a road cut with exposed gravel on both sides.

ROCKHOUNDING

This location sports a large variety of material: agatized shells, petrified wood including some palm wood, agates, jasper, and flint. Most of the pieces are tumbler size, but a few larger specimens can be found.

Do not limit yourselves to this single location. The entire US 83 from Salineño to Zapata is covered in agatized material. Make many stops.

66. Paradise Point Jasper, Flint, and Agate

See map on page 164.

Land type: South Texas brush country; mesquite, cactus, small oaks, and bunch grass; brushy sloping land toward the reservoir

GPS: 26.864235 / -99.2810917

Elevation: 372 feet

Best time of year: Late fall, winter, spring, early summer

Land manager: Falcon Reservoir Water Authority and the Texas Department of Transportation

Material: Agate, jasper, flint, petrified wood

Tools: Geological hammer, garden shovel, short handle rake, spray bottle

Vehicle type: Good highway all the way. 2-wheel drive is sufficient.

The collecting extends down the gravel road.

Precautions and restrictions: Parking can be tight. Pull well off the pavement. If you cannot pull off the pavement, drive on until you can and walk back. Use your warning flashers. Watch for snakes, and carry and use a snake stick when the temperature is above 45°F.

Accommodations: Nice camping at Falcon Lake State Park or Falcon City Park. The sites range from full hookups to water-only tenting and small RV sites. There also are quite a few commercial RV parks and campgrounds in area. Also there are hotels and motels in Zapata and Roma.

SPECIAL ATTRACTIONS

Excellent fishing is in Falcon Lake. There are a number of bass tournaments on the lake every year. Eight- to 10-pound fish are relatively common. Fishing for catfish is excellent. A boat is usually needed during the day, but catfish can be caught from the bank in the early morning and evening. Sunfish are abundant and not only a great attraction for children but can also make for a great dinner.

The animal sanctuary at Salineño offers great opportunities to observe birds, butterflies, and other wildlife.

A great variety of tumblers here

The Zapata County Museum of History is very entertaining and educational.

On the Mexican side of the border, the ruins of the original house of Emiliano Zapata can be visited. He was one of Mexico's most iconic revolutionaries. It has been set up as a museum in the village of Cuautla in the municipality of Ayala.

FINDING THE SITE

Zapata is a city in Zapata County along the Rio Grande. It is about 200 miles south of San Antonio, and it takes about three and a half hours to drive there. In downtown Zapata from the junction of US 83 and Zapata CR 496, turn west on Zapata CR 496 and travel 2.4 miles. At the junction of Texas Farm Road 3074 turn south (left) on this road and drive 1.7 miles. There is a sign here that says the pavement ends.

ROCKHOUNDING

There is a wide expanse at the parking area and a dirt road leading down to the reservoir. You will find plenty of material here. Or you can walk down the road toward the water. The road looked rough the short distance we walked. If you want to drive, a four-wheel drive is recommended. If the water is low, there are some very sizable pieces. Each piece has to be chipped to see what you have. Along the road there are generally smaller pieces, but the patterns and colors are more obvious. You will find agate, jasper, flint, and petrified wood including palm wood.

67. North of Zapata Agate and Petrified Wood North

See map on page 164.

Land type: South Texas brush country; mesquite, cactus, small oaks, and bunch grass; rolling hills, open land

GPS: 26.9514367 / -99.339797

Elevation: 434 feet

Best time of year: Late fall, winter, spring, early summer

Land manager: Texas Department of Transportation

Material: Agate, jasper, petrified wood, flint

Tools: Geological hammer, garden shovel, short handle rake, spray bottle

Vehicle type: Good highway all the way. 2-wheel drive is sufficient.

Precautions and restrictions: Parking can be tight. Pull well off the pavement. If you cannot pull off the pavement, drive on until you can and walk back. Use your warning flashers. Watch for snakes and carry and use a snake stick when the temperature is above 45°F.

The north of Zapata site

Accommodations: Nice camping at Falcon Lake State Park or Falcon City Park. The sites range from full hookups to water-only tenting and small RV sites. There also are quite a few commercial RV parks and campgrounds in the area. Also there are hotels and motels in Zapata and Roma.

SPECIAL ATTRACTIONS

Excellent fishing is in Falcon Lake. There are a number of bass tournaments on the lake every year. Eight- to 10-pound fish are relatively common. Fishing for catfish is excellent. A boat is usually needed during the day, but catfish can be caught from the bank in the early morning and evening. Sunfish are abundant and not only a great attraction for children but can also make for a great dinner.

The animal sanctuary at Salineño offers great opportunities to observe birds, butterflies, and other wildlife. The river front, right in the rockhounding area, offers great fishing for catfish, carp, sunfish, and largemouth bass.

The Zapata County Museum of History is very entertaining and educational.

On the Mexican side of the border, the ruins of the original house of Emiliano Zapata can be visited. He was one of Mexico's most iconic

Very attractive petrified wood and agate

revolutionaries. It has been set up as a museum in the village of Cuautla in the municipality of Ayala.

FINDING THE SITE

Zapata is a city in Zapata County along the Rio Grande. It is about 200 miles south of San Antonio, and it takes about three and a half hours to drive there. From downtown Zapata at the junction of TX 16 and US 83, drive north on US 83 for 5.3 miles. If you look up the hillside, you will see an old roadside picnic area, which is now closed. The location is directly below the picnic area.

ROCKHOUNDING

Folks used to collect right in the picnic area, but it is now closed. However the road cut directly below is full of material. You will find jasper, flint, agate, and petrified wood including some palm wood. The pieces are mostly small, but with diligence some nice slicers can be picked up.

68. South of Laredo Agate, Petrified Wood, and Jasper

Land type: South Texas brush country; mesquite, cactus, small oaks, and bunch grass; rolling hills with brush
GPS: 27.392665 / -99.476002
Elevation: 503 feet
Best time of year: Late fall, winter, spring, early summer
Land manager: Texas Department of Transportation
Material: Agate, jasper, petrified wood, flint
Tools: Geological hammer, garden shovel, short handle rake, spray bottle
Vehicle type: Good highway all the way. 2-wheel drive is sufficient.
Precautions and restrictions: Parking can be tight. Pull well off the pavement. If you cannot pull off the pavement, drive on until you can and walk back. Use your warning flashers. Watch for snakes, and carry and use a snake stick when the temperature is above 45°F.

Image of the site

Sites 61–62, 68–70

Accommodations: Lake Casa Blanca International State Park offers fine camping opportunities. They have 11 full hookup sites and 56 electric and water-only sites. Laredo is a very visited city, and therefore has many fine commercial RV resorts and campgrounds. There also are a lot of motels and hotels.

Attractive material from this site

SPECIAL ATTRACTIONS

Fishing in Lake Casa Blanca is good. The premier species is largemouth bass, but there are excellent numbers of catfish that include channel cats, blue cats, and flathead cats. The flatheads and blue cats grow to prodigious sizes in this lake. Fish over 20 pounds are caught most years. There also are good numbers of crappie, carp, and a few hybrid striped bass.

If you are fishing from the shore within the state park, no license is needed.

The park also offers geocaching, trails for hiking and biking, playgrounds, and courts for various sports.

Laredo offers a number of museums. Whether you choose the Republic of the Rio Grande Museum, the Laredo Water Museum, the Imaginarium of South Texas Museum, or the Border Heritage Museum, a fine outing will be had by all.

FINDING THE SITE

Laredo is a city and county seat of Webb County, which is along the banks of the Rio Grande River. It is about 160 miles southwest of San Antonio, and it takes about two and half hours to drive the distance. From Laredo at the junction of US 83 and TX 20, drive south on US 83 for 1.1 mile. You will see an eroded area on the side of the road.

ROCKHOUNDING

We found enough here to make the stop worthwhile. However, the material is not nearly as plentiful as it is around Zapata. The take includes petrified wood, agates, jasper, and flint. There are plenty of small pieces as float, but digging will probably produce larger pieces.

69. Laredo US 59 Agate, Jasper, and Petrified Wood

See map on page 180.

Land type: South Texas brush country; mesquite, cactus, small oaks, and bunch grass; flat, brushy desert

GPS: 27.5505557 / -99.4062613

Elevation: 310.9 feet

Best time of year: Late fall to late spring

Land manager: Texas Department of Transportation

Material: Agate, jasper, petrified wood

Tools: Geological hammer, small short handle shovel, rake, spray bottle

Vehicle type: Good road. 2-wheel drive is OK.

Precautions and restrictions: Park well off the road and use your flashers.

Accommodations: Lake Casa Blanca International State Park offers fine camping opportunities. It has 11 full hookup sites and 56 electric and water-only sites. Laredo is a very visited city, and therefore has many fine commercial RV resorts and campgrounds. There also are a lot of motels and hotels.

Nice pull-off here

Well-preserved fossils here

SPECIAL ATTRACTIONS

Fishing in Lake Casa Blanca is good. The premier species is largemouth bass, but there are excellent numbers of catfish that include channel cats, blue cats, and flathead cats. The flatheads and blue cats grow to prodigious sizes in this lake. Fish over 20 pounds are caught most years. There also are good numbers of crappie, carp, and a few hybrid striped bass.

If you are fishing from the shore within the state park, no license is needed.

The park also offers geocaching, trails for hiking and biking, playgrounds, and courts for various sports.

Laredo offers a number of museums. Whether you choose the Republic of the Rio Grande Museum, the Laredo Water Museum, the Imaginarium of South Texas Museum, or the Border Heritage Museum, a fine outing will be had by all.

FINDING THE SITE

Laredo is a city in and the county seat of Webb County, which is along the banks of the Rio Grande River. It is about 160 miles southwest of San Antonio, and it takes about two and half hours to drive the distance. This site is located in northeast Laredo near Casa Blanca State Park. From the junction

Nice piece of chocolate agate from this site

of US 59 and TX 20 (Bob Bullock Loop Road), travel northeast on US 59 for 3 miles. The site is on the east side of the road.

ROCKHOUNDING

Numerous rocks are visible as float. We found some very nice pieces of petrified wood, agate, and marine fossils. The agate had a wide range of colors. Some was rather clear with interesting inclusion and should make up into fine jewelry-quality cabs.

Do not limit yourselves to this location alone. There is material all along this route for many miles. Make a number of stops.

70. Bonanza Hills Petrified Wood and Jasper

See map on page 180.

Land type: South Texas brush country; mesquite, cactus, small oaks, and bunch grass; rolling desert and scrub

GPS: 27.7723867 / -99.4457183

Elevation: 739 feet

Best time of year: Late fall through the middle of spring. It can be very hot in the summer.

Land manager: Texas Department of Transportation

Material: Petrified wood, jasper

Tools: Geological hammer, spray bottle, short handle rake, small garden shovel

Vehicle type: Good highway. 2-wheel drive will work.

Precautions and restrictions: Be very careful pulling in here. There is a lot of 18-wheeler truck traffic. They drive very fast. Pull far off the road. Be careful getting out of your vehicle and use your flashers.

Accommodations: Lake Casa Blanca International State Park offers fine camping opportunities. They have 11 full hookup sites and 56 electric and water-only

Construction here unearthed some nice material.

Petrified wood from this site

sites. Laredo is a highly visited city, and therefore has many fine commercial RV resorts and campgrounds. There also are a lot of motels and hotels. Fishing in Lake Casa Blanca is good.

SPECIAL ATTRACTIONS

Fishing in Lake Casa Blanca is good. The premier species is large-mouth bass, but there are excellent numbers of catfish that include channel cats, blue cats, and flat-head cats. The flatheads and blue cats grow to prodigious sizes in this lake. Fish over 20 pounds are caught most years. There also are good numbers of crappie, carp, and a few hybrid striped bass.

If you are fishing from the shore within the state park, no license is needed.

The park also offers geocaching, trails for hiking and biking, playgrounds, and courts for various sports.

Laredo offers a number of museums. Whether you choose the Republic of the Rio Grande Museum, the Laredo Water Museum, the Imaginarium of South Texas Museum, or the Border Heritage Museum, a fine outing will be had by all.

FINDING THE SITE

Laredo is a city in and the county seat of Webb County, which is along the banks of the Rio Grande River. It is about 160 miles southwest of San Antonio, and it takes about two and half hours to drive the distance. This site is located about 10–15 miles north of the city of Laredo. From the junction of US 83 with TX 255, travel south on US 83 for 3.6 miles. Just past the Bonanza Hills housing development, there is a good pull-off on the east side (right of the road if you are coming from Laredo).

ROCKHOUNDING

We kept to the east side of the road because it was dangerous crossing. We found jasper in multiple shades of red, green, and yellow. There was a good amount of petrified wood. Some of this included palm wood, but it is difficult to identify until cut.

71. US 83 Catarina Picnic Area

Land type: South Texas brush country; mesquite, cactus, small oaks, and bunch grass; desert with some scrub
GPS: 28.3755992 / -99.6482839
Elevation: 612 feet
Best time of year: Late fall, winter, early spring. It can be very hot in the summer.
Land manager: Texas Department of Transportation
Material: Petrified wood, jasper
Tools: Geological hammer, spray bottle, short handle rake, garden shovel
Vehicle type: Good highway. 2-wheel drive is sufficient.
Precautions and restrictions: This is a good pullout but be careful. If the temperature is above 45°F, watch for snakes. Always use a snake stick before stepping near brush.
Accommodations: Casa Blanca International State Park offers fine camping opportunities. They have 11 full hookup sites and 56 electric and water-only sites. Laredo is a very visited city, and therefore has many fine commercial RV resorts and campgrounds. There also are a lot of motels and hotels.

Image of the collecting area

Sites 71–73

Assortment of petrified wood from this area

SPECIAL ATTRACTIONS

Fishing in Lake Casa Blanca is good. The premier species is largemouth bass, but there are excellent numbers of catfish that include channel cats, blue cats, and flathead cats. The flatheads and blue cats grow to prodigious sizes in this lake. Fish over 20 pounds are caught most years. There also are good numbers of crappie, carp, and a few hybrid striped bass.

If you are fishing from the shore within the state park, no license is needed.

The park also offers geocaching, trails for hiking and biking, playgrounds, and courts for various sports.

Laredo offers a number of museums. Whether you choose the Republic of the Rio Grande Museum, the Laredo Water Museum, the Imaginarium of South Texas Museum, or the Border Heritage Museum, a fine outing will be had by all.

FINDING THE SITE

Laredo is a city in and the county seat of Webb County, which is along the banks of the Rio Grande River. It is about 160 miles southwest of San Antonio, and it takes about two and half hours to drive the distance. Carrizo Springs is about 82 miles north of Laredo with an hour and a half drive time. This site is located just south of the town of Carrizo Springs. From the junction of US 277 and US 83, travel south on US 83 for 16.8 miles to a picnic area on the east (left) side of the road. Park in the picnic area.

ROCKHOUNDING

There is lots of petrified wood scattered everywhere. Palm wood is in the mix but may be difficult to identify until it is taken home and cut. There is a lot of yellow jasper and some red. Keep your eyes open for the brown jasper. Much of it has some very attractive red inclusions. This is the prize from this site. We found the best material close to the road.

72. East of Eagle Pass Petrified Wood and Fossils

See map on page 188.

Land type: South Texas brush country; mesquite, cactus, small oaks, and bunch grass; hilly desert with some scrub

GPS: 28.6611356 / -100. 2630561

Elevation: 924 feet

Best time of year: Late fall, winter through early spring. It can be very hot during the summer.

Land manager: Texas Department of Transportation

Material: Petrified wood, fossils, jasper, agate

Tools: Geological hammer, short handle rake, garden shovel, spray bottle

Vehicle type: Good highway. 2-wheel drive is sufficient.

Precautions and restrictions: Busy highway. Pull well off the road and use flashers. Snakes are present during warmer periods. Use a snake stick before stepping near or on brush. Look under each piece you pick up for insects and arachnids.

Image of site

Accommodations: There are numerous commercial campgrounds and RV parks in Eagle Pass. Motels and hotels are also plentiful.

SPECIAL ATTRACTIONS

Lucky Eagle Casino Hotel is the only casino in Texas. They feature numerous slot machines including one that eats pennies.

Fort Duncan Park is home to the Fort Duncan Museum, which commemorates the First United States Infantry encampment set up back in 1849. Listed on the National Register of Historic Places, the museum displays exhibits on the history of the fort and is located inside the original army headquarters building.

There is good fishing at Maverick County Lake. Besides fishing by boat or off the pier, the park also features a 1.5-mile walking and jogging trail, playground equipment, softball fields, and a picnic area.

FINDING THE SITE

Eagle Pass is a city in and the county seat of Maverick County. This city is about 150 miles from San Antonio, and it takes about two and a half hours to drive the distance. This location is about 10 miles southeast of Eagle Pass. From Carrizo Springs at the junction of US 83 and US 277, travel northwest on US 277 for 28.7 miles. The site is on the east (right) side.

Typical fossil rock found here

If you are coming from Eagle Pass: From the junction of US 277 and Texas Loop 480, travel southeast on US 277 for 10.2 miles.

ROCKHOUNDING

There is a lot of petrified wood here as well as jasper. We also found some small pieces of clear agate with interesting inclusions. A bonus find at this site was various marine fossils.

73. Near Quemado Petrified Wood and Fossils

See map on page 188.
Land type: South Texas brush country; mesquite, cactus, small oaks, and bunch grass; hilly desert with some scrub
GPS: 289252974/ -100.6146257
Elevation: 245.9 feet
Best time of year: Late fall, winter through early spring
Land manager: Texas Department of Transportation
Material: Petrified wood and marine fossils
Tools: Geological hammer, short handle rake, garden shovel, spray bottle
Vehicle type: Good highway. 2-wheel drive is OK.
Precautions and restrictions: The road could be busy, and the speed limit is high. Be careful pulling off and use your flashers. Snakes active when the temperature is above 45°F.
Accommodations: There are numerous commercial campgrounds and RV parks in Eagle Pass. Motels and hotels are also plentiful.

View of picnic area collecting site

Typical material found here

SPECIAL ATTRACTIONS

Lucky Eagle Casino Hotel is the only casino in Texas. They feature numerous slot machines including one that eats pennies.

Fort Duncan Park is home to the Fort Duncan Museum, which commemorates the First United States Infantry encampment set up back in 1849. Listed on the National Register of Historic Places, the museum displays exhibits on the history of the fort and is located inside the original army headquarters building.

There is good fishing at Maverick County Lake. Besides fishing by boat or off the pier, the park also features a 1.5-mile walking and jogging trail, playground equipment, softball fields, and a picnic area.

FINDING THE SITE

Eagle Pass is a city in and the county seat of Maverick County. This city is about 150 miles from San Antonio, and it takes about two and a half hours to drive the distance. This site is located north of Eagle Pass just south of the small town of Quemado. If you are coming from the northern end of Eagle Pass, from the junction of US 277 and US Business Route 277, drive on US 277 north for 15.8 miles.

From Quemado, from the junction of US 227 and Texas Farm Road 1591, proceed south on US 277 to the picnic area on the east (left) side of the road. Pull into the picnic area and drive to the south end.

ROCKHOUNDING

There is petrified wood and some marine fossils located around the site. It appears as though they are most plentiful close to the road. You will also find flint of various shades.

WEST TEXAS

Over geological time, West Texas has had a violent volcanic history. This made it the premier region in the Lone Star State for rock hounds.

This area contains the most beautiful agates the state has to offer. Upper and Lower Cretaceous fossils are quite widespread and abundant. Isolated discoveries of sard, chrysoprase, celestite, chrysocolla, and very attractive quartz crystals are a good possibility here. Some geodes have been found as well as a variety of petrified woods including palm wood. Cinnabar, galena, limonite, peridot, and hematite are also possible finds. Please don't misunderstand the above, as they are rare finds but also a possibility.

In the past there were a number of ranches in the Big Bend area that allowed rock hounds to collect on a pay-to-collect basis. As of this writing, these have, for the most part, discontinued the practice. These situations change over time. So keep yourselves up to date on that status if you would enjoy that type of rockhounding.

All the above said, roadside rock hunting in the region is excellent. The road cuts are usually quite large due to the mountainous nature of the region. These can provide large exposures of material not otherwise found at the surface.

Again, like a lot of the Lone Star State, the summers can be very hot. So carry lots of water and sunscreen. Many prefer winter to collect here, but it can be done anytime as long as you are prepared.

74. South of Del Rio Petrified Wood

Land type: South Texas brush country; mesquite, cactus, small oaks, and bunch grass; desert with some scrub and prickly pears
GPS: 29.3097205 / -100.7954841
Elevation: 1,086 feet
Best time of year: Late fall, winter, early spring. It can be very hot in summer.
Land manager: Texas Department of Transportation
Material: Petrified wood, agate, flint, jasper
Tools: Geological hammer, short handle rake, garden shovel, spray bottle
Vehicle type: Good highway. 2-wheel drive is OK.
Precautions and restrictions: The road could be busy, and the speed limit is high. Be careful pulling off and use your flashers. Snakes are active when the temperature is above 45°F.
Accommodations: The Army Corps of Engineers runs 5 campgrounds at the Amistad National Recreation Area. These are Governors Landing, Rough Canyon,

View from the pull-off at this site

Sites 74–77

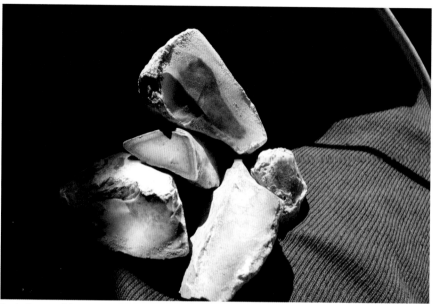
Typical material from this area

San Pedro, Spur 406, and 277 North. There are no reservations. They are on a first-come, first-served basis. There also are a number of RV resorts as well as fish camps. Motels and hotels can be found in and around Del Rio.

SPECIAL ATTRACTIONS

Fishing in Amistad Lake is excellent. Largemouth bass anglers travel from all corners of the world because this lake produces bass of very prodigious sizes.

Besides the largemouth bass, this water also holds smallmouth bass; channel, blue, and flathead catfish; white and black crappie; a good run of white bass; and some striped bass and their hybrids.

There are a number of guide services who take folks out for a fee, and fishing from the shoreline is certainly productive.

Besides fishing, bird watching is a popular activity, and there are a number hiking and biking trails around the lake.

The Whitehead Memorial Museum is certainly worth a visit if you are interested in the history of the area. Whitehead Memorial Museum's mission is to preserve artifacts that reflect the early cultures, history, and economics of Del Rio and Val Verde County.

FINDING THE SITE

Del Rio is a city in and the county seat of Val Verde County. It is located on the banks of the Rio Grande River and is about 152 miles west of San Antonio. It takes about two and a half hours to drive to Del Rio from San Antonio. This site is just south of Del Rio. From the southern end of Del Rio, from the junction of US 277 and Texas Loop 79, also called Dr. Fermin Calderon Blvd., head south on US 277 for 22 miles to the site, which is on the east side of the road.

Quemado is about 36 miles southeast of Del Rio, and it takes about 35 minutes to drive there. From Quemado, from the cross roads of US 277 and Texas Farm Road 1591, drive north 26.9 miles on US 277.

ROCKHOUNDING

This area is perfect for collecting small pieces of petrified wood. It is not very abundant, but there's enough to keep collectors happy, especially if you want lots of tumblers.

75. Del Rio Fossils

See map on page 197.

Land type: South Texas brush country; mesquite, cactus, small oaks, and bunch grass; desert with some scrub and cacti, many of them prickly pears; slightly hilly

GPS: 29.4520045 / -100.9313524

Elevation: 1,234 feet

Best time of year: Late fall, winter, early spring. It can be very hot in summer.

Land manager: Texas Department of Transportation

Material: Marine fossils, some chalcedony

Tools: Geological hammer, short rake, garden shovel, spray bottle

Vehicle type: Good highway. 2-wheel drive is OK.

Precautions and restrictions: The road can be busy, and the speed limit is high. Be careful pulling off and use your flashers. Snakes are active when the temperature is above 45°F.

Accommodations: The Army Corp of Engineers run 5 campgrounds at the Amistad National Recreation Area. These are Governors Landing, Rough Canyon, San Pedro, Spur 406, and 277 North. There are no reservations. They are on a first-come, first-served basis.

View of collecting area

SPECIAL ATTRACTIONS

Fishing in Amistad Lake is excellent. Largemouth bass anglers travel from all corners of the world because this lake produces bass of very prodigious sizes.

Fossil bivalve from this area

Besides the largemouth bass, this water also holds smallmouth bass; channel, blue, and flathead catfish; white and black crappie; a good run of white bass; and some striped bass and their hybrids.

There are a number of guide services who take folks out for a fee, and fishing from the shoreline is certainly productive.

Besides fishing, bird watching is a popular activity, and there are a number of hiking and biking trails around the lake.

The Whitehead Memorial Museum is certainly worth a visit if you are interested in the history of the area. Whitehead Memorial Museum's mission is to preserve artifacts that reflect the early cultures, history, and economics of Del Rio and Val Verde County.

FINDING THE SITE

Del Rio is a city in and the county seat of Val Verde County. It is located on the banks of the Rio Grande River and is about 152 miles west of San Antonio. It takes about two and a half hours to drive to Del Rio from San Antonio. From the junction of US 90, also called Veteran's Boulevard, and Murphy gas station at Walmart, which is on the north side of town, drive north for 4.5 miles on US 90 to a very large road cut.

ROCKHOUNDING

The geology of the area shows Lower Cretaceous limestone. This limestone, also known as Buda limestone, is very fossiliferous. The collecting is on both sides of the road. In a short time we collected some intact brachiopods, and a lot of clams were evident. Nice banded limestone can be picked up. This takes a good polish. Also present is some chalcedony as well as a bit of petrified wood.

76. Comstock Fossils

Image of wall of road cut

See map on page 197.
Land type: South Texas brush country; mesquite, cactus, small oaks, and bunch grass; desert with some scrub and prickly pears; slightly hilly
GPS: 29.5776233 / -101.070905
Elevation: 1,379 feet
Best time of year: Late fall, winter, early spring. It can be very hot in summer.
Land manager: Texas Department of Transportation
Material: Marine fossils, banded limestone
Tools: Geological hammer, short handle rake, garden shovel, spray bottle
Vehicle type: Good highway. 2-wheel drive is OK.
Precautions and restrictions: The road can be busy, and the speed limit is high. Be careful pulling off and use your flashers. Snakes are active when the temperature is above 45°F.

Pretty banded limestone

Accommodations: Seminole Canyon State Park and Historic Site offers a variety of camping possibilities. They have sites with electric and water as well as water-only locations.

SPECIAL ATTRACTIONS

Seminole Canyon State Park and Historic Site is certainly worth a visit. It features pictograms dating back to well before Europeans came to the Americas.

Twelve thousand years ago, early migrants came to the canyon to hunt mammoth, camel, bison, and horse. It is believed that these folks eventually killed off most of the large mammals and moved on.

Other people showed up around 7,000 years ago and hunted small animals and gathered plants from the desert. They were the ones who produced the pictograms.

The park service conducts tours to the rock shelters that housed these folks and where they produced their pictograms. These programs have to be signed up for in advance.

FINDING THE SITE

Comstock is about 188 miles a little north and west of San Antonio. It takes almost 3 hours to drive between the two cities. If driving from Comstock,

Fossils in limestone at Comstock

from the junction of TX 163 and US 90, head south on US 90 for 10.6 miles to a very large road cut.

This site is about halfway between Comstock and Lake Amistad.

Del Rio is a city in and the county seat of Val Verde County. It is located on the banks of the Rio Grande River and is about 152 miles west of San Antonio. It takes about two and a half hours to drive to Del Rio from San Antonio. If you are heading to this site from Del Rio, at the junction of US 90 and Texas Spur Road 406, go north on US 90 for 15 miles.

ROCKHOUNDING

This road cut extends for a half mile. We made only one stop but are quite sure material can be found throughout it. We found marine fossils, both casts as well as impressions. Again, a very nice banded limestone is found here. It takes a fine polish.

77. Pecos River Fossils

Pecos River road cut

See map on page 197.
Land type: South Texas brush country; mesquite, cactus, small oaks, and bunch grass; desert with some scrub and prickly pears; hilly desert
GPS: 29.70440681 / -101.3458491
Elevation: 1,454 feet
Best time of year: Late fall, winter, early spring. It can be very hot in summer.
Land manager: Texas Department of Transportation
Material: Marine fossils
Tools: Geological hammer, short handle rake, garden shovel, spray bottle
Vehicle type: Good highway. 2-wheel drive is OK.
Precautions and restrictions: The road can be busy, and the speed limit is high. Be careful pulling off and use your flashers. Snakes active when the temperature is above 45°F.
Accommodations: Seminole Canyon State Park and Historic Site offers a variety of camping possibilities. They have sites with electric and water as well as water-only locations.

Abundant fossils in these rocks

SPECIAL ATTRACTIONS

Seminole Canyon State Park and Historic Site is certainly worth a visit. It features pictograms dating back to well before Europeans came to the Americas.

Twelve thousand years ago, early migrants came to the canyon to hunt mammoth, camel, bison, and horse. It is believed that these folks eventually killed off most of the large mammals and moved on.

Other people showed up around 7,000 years ago and hunted small animals and gathered plants from the desert. They were the ones that produced the pictograms.

The park service conducts tours to the rock shelters that housed these folks and where they produced their pictograms. These programs have to be signed up for in advance.

FINDING THE SITE

Langtry is an unincorporated community in Val Verde County. It is 215 miles a bit north and west from San Antonio. It takes about three and a half hours to drive the distance. This site is located just south of the Pecos River Bridge. If approaching from the north, in Langtry at the south end of the Texas Loop 25, also called Langtry Loop, and US 90, drive 16.7 miles on US 90 to the southern end of the Pecos River Bridge. You can park here or drive another quarter of a mile to another large parking area.

ROCKHOUNDING

The area is dissected with Cretaceous limestone. This formation is very fossiliferous. This area has lots of marine fossils. Most of these will be found in the yellow-colored rock. Some are also located in the gray rock.

78. South of Dryden Petrified Wood

Land type: Dryden sits on the boundary of two different Texas land types and exhibits characteristics of both. South Texas brush country has mesquite, cactus, small oaks, and bunch grass. The Edward's Plateau and Hill Country show highly variable vegetation: oak, cedar, mesquite, woodlands, grass prairies, and cypress waterways. Here the desert is becoming more varied with cacti, yucca, mesquite, and other vegetation.

GPS: 29.95059 / -101.9939417

Elevation: 2,122 feet

Best time of year: Late fall, winter, early spring. It can be very hot in summer.

Land manager: Texas Department of Transportation

Material: Petrified wood mixed with agate, flint, jasper

Tools: Geological hammer, short rake, garden shovel, spray bottle

Vehicle type: Good highway. 2-wheel drive is OK.

Search near the fence line.

Sites 78–83

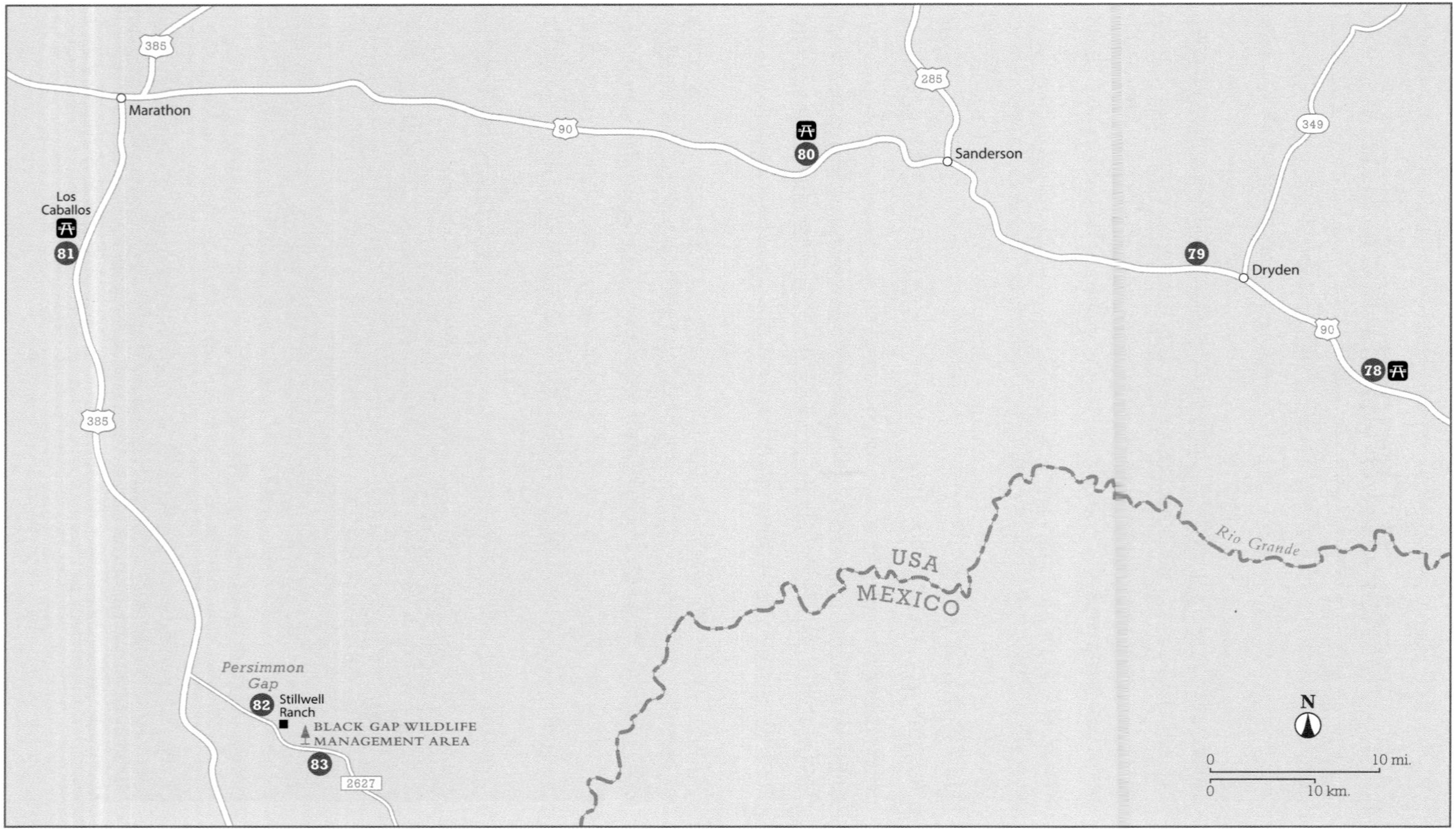

N

10 mi.

10 km.

Rio Grande

USA
MEXICO

Dryden

Sanderson

Marathon

Los
Caballos

Persimmon
Gap

Stillwell
Ranch

BLACK GAP WILDLIFE
MANAGEMENT AREA

349

90

285

90

385

385

2627

78

79

80

81

82

83

Perhaps a limb cast or fossil bone from this area

Precautions and restrictions: The road could be busy, and the speed limit is high. Be careful pulling off into the picnic area. Snakes are active when the temperature is above 45°F.
Accommodations: Seminole Canyon State Park and Historic Site offers a variety of camping possibilities. They have sites with electric and water as well as water-only locations.

SPECIAL ATTRACTIONS

Seminole Canyon State Park and Historic Site is certainly worth a visit. It features pictograms dating back to well before Europeans came to the Americas.

Twelve thousand years ago, early migrants came to the canyon to hunt mammoth, camel, bison, and horse. It is believed that these folks eventually killed off most of the large mammals and moved on.

Other people showed up around 7,000 years ago and hunted small animals and gathered plants from the desert. They were the ones that produced the pictograms.

The park service conducts tours to the rock shelters that housed these folks and where they produced their pictograms. These programs have to be signed up for in advance.

FINDING THE SITE

Dryden is an unincorporated community in south central Terrell County. It is about 255 miles a little north and west from San Antonio with a drive time of about 4 hours and 10 minutes. From Dryden at the junction of US 90 and TX 349, travel south on US 90 for 10.1 miles to a picnic area on the east side the road.

ROCKHOUNDING

The collecting was best at the northeast end of the picnic area. Look for material from before the posts to the end of the picnic area. There are lots of small pieces, and larger ones should be chopped to see if there is a hidden treasure inside. We found a number of very-well-preserved limb casts and what we suspect is fossilized bone.

79. North of Dryden Petrified Wood

See map on page 208.

Land type: Dryden sits on the boundary of two different Texas land types and exhibits characteristics of both. South Texas brush country has mesquite, cactus, small oaks, and bunch grass. The Edward's Plateau and Hill Country show highly variable vegetation: oak, cedar, mesquite, woodlands, grass prairies, and cypress waterways. Here the desert is becoming more varied with cacti, yucca, mesquite, and other vegetation.

GPS: 30.05224 / -102.167235

Elevation: 2,300 feet

Best time of year: All year. It can be very hot in summer and snow covered in winter.

Land manager: Texas Department of Transportation

Material: Petrified wood, jasper, flint, agate

Tools: Geological hammer, short rake, garden shovel, spray bottle

Vehicle type: Good highway. 2-wheel drive is OK.

Image of collecting area

Typical material from this site

Precautions and restrictions: The road can be busy, and the speed limit is high. Be careful pulling off and use your flashers. Snakes are active when the temperature is above 45°F.

Accommodations: Seminole Canyon State Park and Historic Site offers a variety of camping possibilities. They have sites with electric and water as well as water-only locations.

SPECIAL ATTRACTIONS

Seminole Canyon State Park and Historic Site is certainly worth a visit. It features pictograms dating back to well before Europeans came to the Americas.

Twelve thousand years ago, early migrants came to the canyon to hunt mammoth, camel, bison, and horse. It is believed that these folks eventually killed off most of the large mammals and moved on.

Other people showed up around 7,000 years ago and hunted small animals and gathered plants from the desert. They were the ones that produced the pictograms.

The park service conducts tours to the rock shelters that housed these folks and where they produced their pictograms. These programs have to be signed up for in advance.

FINDING THE SITE

Dryden is an unincorporated community in south central Terrell County. It is about 255 miles a little north of west from San Antonio with a drive time of about 4 hours and 10 minutes. From Dryden at the junction of US 90 and TX 349, head north on US 90 for 3.2 miles.

ROCKHOUNDING

The rocks at this location are mainly cherty and fossiliferous. These are a result of the erosion of the Lower Cretaceous Edwards limestone. There is plenty of material here. We found a large variety of agates, flint, and petrified wood. We also believe that a few of the pieces kept were specimens of fossilized bone. They were well agatized. However, they may be limb casts. We are working on the definitive identification of these specimens.

80. Sanderson Petrified Wood

See map on page 208.

Land type: The Edward's Plateau and Hill Country show highly variable vegetation: oak, cedar, mesquite, woodlands, grass prairies, and cypress waterways. This area is more mountainous, there are lots of buttes in the area, and the high desert environment is evident.

GPS: 30.1434207 / -102.5431219

Elevation: 3,214 feet

Best time of year: All year. It can be very hot in summer and snow covered in winter.

Land manager: Texas Department of Transportation

Material: Petrified wood, agate, chalcedony.

Tools: Geological hammer, short rake, garden shovel, spray bottle

Vehicle type: Good highway. 2-wheel drive is OK.

Precautions and restrictions: You are parked in a picnic area. Just be sure not to cross the fence line onto private property. Snakes are active when the temperature reaches 45°F.

Image of collecting area

Typical material from this site

Accommodations: Seminole Canyon State Park and Historic Site offers a variety of camping possibilities. They have sites with electric and water as well as water-only locations.

SPECIAL ATTRACTIONS

Seminole Canyon State Park and Historic Site is certainly worth a visit. It features pictograms dating back to well before Europeans came to the Americas.

Twelve thousand years ago, early migrants came to the canyon to hunt mammoth, camel, bison, and horse. It is believed that these folks eventually killed off most of the large mammals and moved on.

Other people showed up around 7,000 years ago and hunted small animals and gathered plants from the desert. They were the ones that produced the pictograms.

The park service conducts tours to the rock shelters that housed these folks and where they produced their pictograms. These programs have to signed up for in advance.

There are a few motels in Sanderson and Marathon.

FINDING THE SITE

From Sanderson at the junction of US 90 and US 285, go north on US 90 for 9.4 miles. You'll find a picnic area on the east (right) side of the road.

ROCKHOUNDING

Many years ago while traveling to Big Bend, we stopped at the picnic area for lunch. Much to our surprise it was covered with all kinds of material. This is the first time we've returned to this location and, again, a big surprise. The place still sports a lot of petrified wood, some of which is palm wood, a variety of agates, and other chalcedony. We also picked up fossilized bone. Be sure to stop and take a look here if you are passing through.

81. Los Caballos Picnic Area

See map on page 208.

Land type: The Edward's Plateau and Hill Country show highly variable vegetation: oak, cedar, mesquite, woodlands, grass prairies, and cypress waterways. This area is more mountainous, there are lots of buttes in the area, and the high desert environment is evident.

GPS: 30.06655 / -103.2744835

Elevation: 3,650 feet

Best time of year: Late fall, winter, early spring. The summers can be very hot.

Land manager: Texas Department of Transportation

Material: Jasper, petrified wood, agates, and green sard

Tools: Geological hammer, short handle rake, garden shovel, spray bottle

Vehicle type: Good highway. 2-wheel drive is OK.

Precautions and restrictions: Snakes are active here when the temperature is above 45°F. The rest area has ample room for a number of vehicles and is a popular boondocking location. Just make sure you leave enough room for folks to drive past your vehicle.

It's a small area so be sure to leave enough space for others.

Sard and other material from this location

Accommodations: The Stillwell Ranch offers RV campsites and is within a few miles of this location. The Big Bend National Park hosts a number of campsites. Reservations are suggested as it has become a very visited park in recent years. In addition, there are a number of private campgrounds in and around Marathon. Marathon, Sanderson, and Alpine also have a number of motels, hotels, and resorts. Big Bend National Park also has a very nice upscale lodge.

SPECIAL ATTRACTIONS

Big Bend National Park is well known for hiking trails. These range from very easy to very strenuous. Many folks travel to this park for the great bird watching and wildlife observation. The park boasts a hot pool sitting right on the banks of the Rio Grande River. You can drive to within a quarter mile of the pool. The rangers offer bird-watching tours as well as geology talks. Stargazing is also a very popular activity here because air pollution is very low. The park offers astronomy talks at night.

FINDING THE SITE

Marathon is a census-designated place in Brewster County. It is about 370 miles west of San Antonio and takes about 5 hours and 10 minutes to drive the distance. In Marathon, at the junction of US 90 and US 385, take US 385 south for 10.2 miles to a picnic area on the right.

ROCKHOUNDING

When we first came upon this site about 30 years ago, good material littered the area. While this has thinned out over the years, there still is enough to make it a worthwhile stop. There have been reports of chrysoprase being found in the area. We have never found any. The collecting areas are at the north or the south end of the picnic area. Just walk along the right-of-way and you will find agates, jasper, some petrified wood, and other chalcedony including green sard. This might be the material others have mistakenly thought was chrysoprase. Sard is a chalcedony that is used for carving cameos. Most use a sardonyx where there are at least two layers of colors. What we found was not sardonyx since it was solid green as opposed to layered, but it would also be appropriate for carving. It also makes into fine looking cabs.

82. Persimmon Gap Selenite

See map on page 208.
Land type: The Edward's Plateau and Hill Country show highly variable vegetation: oak, cedar, mesquite, woodlands, grass prairies, and cypress waterways. This area is more mountainous, there are lots of buttes in the area, and the high desert environment is evident.
GPS: 29.6518863 / -103.0964555
Elevation: 2,959 feet
Best time of year: Late fall, winter, early spring. The summers can be very hot.
Land manager: Texas Department of Transportation
Material: Selenite, barite, quartz crystals, white flint nodules
Tools: Geological hammer, short rake, garden shovel, spray bottle
Vehicle type: Good highway. 2-wheel drive is OK.
Precautions and restrictions: This spot has its own security. Snakes abound. In fact we did encounter one rattler at the location. Be aware. Parking is difficult. Pull to the side of the road before entering or after passing through the cut. Use your flashers and walk to the display.

The large road cut at Persimmons Gap

Accommodations: The Stillwell Ranch offers RV campsites and is within a few miles of this location. The Big Bend National Park hosts a number of campsites. Reservations are suggested as it has become a very visited park in recent years. In addition, there are a number of private campgrounds in and around Study Butte. Study Butte has a number of motels, hotels, and resorts. There also is a historic hotel within the park.

SPECIAL ATTRACTIONS

Big Bend National Park is well known for hiking trails. These range from very easy to very strenuous. Many folks travel to this park for the great bird watching and wildlife observation. The park boasts a hot pool sitting right on the banks of the Rio Grande River. You can drive to within a quarter mile of the pool. The rangers offer bird-watching tours as well as geology talks. Stargazing is also a very popular activity here because air pollution is very low. The park offers astronomy talks at night.

FINDING THE SITE

Marathon is a census-designated place in Brewster County. It is about 370 miles west of San Antonio and takes about 5 hours and 10 minutes to drive the distance. From Marathon, at the junction of US 90 and US 385, turn

Beautiful crystals in the rocks of the road cut walls

south on US 385 and drive 39 miles. This is the junction of US 385 and Texas Farm Road 2627. This is a couple of miles north of the border of Big Bend National Park. Turn to the southeast on Texas Farm Road 2627. The road cut is 4.8 miles from your turn. It is on top of the highest hill on this road.

ROCKHOUNDING

We included this site to be admired rather than to be destroyed by chiseling. The waterfall of the selenite crystals is on the north (left) side of the road cut. The road cut looks like a sparkling fairy world. This outcropping is varied: delicate selenite bunches, barite roses, white flint, and barite nodules. Some of this contains white quartz crystals.

83. Black Gap Agate, Flint, and Jasper

See map on page 208.

Land type: The Edward's Plateau and Hill Country show highly variable vegetation: oak, cedar, mesquite, woodlands, grass prairies, and cypress waterways. This area is more mountainous, there are lots of buttes in the area, and the high desert environment is evident.

GPS: 29.6306377 / -103.070144

Elevation: 2,685 feet

Best time of year: Late fall, winter, early spring. The summers can be very hot.

Land manager: Texas Department of Transportation

Material: Agate, jasper, flint, petrified wood

Tools: Geological hammer, short rake, garden shovel, spray bottle

Vehicle type: Good highway. 2-wheel drive is OK.

Precautions and restrictions: The road is narrow. and, though it is not very busy, you should pull well off to the side. Use your flashers. Snakes are active when the temperature is above 45°F.

Lots of material here

Nice material from Black Gap

Accommodations: The Stillwell Ranch offers RV campsites and is within a few miles of this location. The Big Bend National Park hosts a number of campsites. Reservations are suggested as it has become a very visited park in recent years. In addition, there are a number of private campgrounds in and around Study Butte. Study Butte has a number of motels, hotels, and resorts. There also is a historic hotel within the park.

SPECIAL ATTRACTIONS

Big Bend National Park is well known for hiking trails. These range from very easy to very strenuous. Many folks travel to this park for the great bird watching and wildlife observation. The park boasts a hot pool sitting right on the banks of the Rio Grande River. You can drive to within a quarter mile of the pool. The rangers offer bird-watching tours as well as geology talks. Stargazing is also a very popular activity here because air pollution is very low. The park offers astronomy talks at night.

FINDING THE SITE

Marathon is a census-designated place in Brewster County. It is about 370 miles west of San Antonio and takes about 5 hours and 10 minutes to drive the distance. This site is located within the Black Gap Wildlife Management Area. From Marathon, at the junction of US 90 and US 385, turn south on US 385 and drive 39 miles. This is the junction of US 385 and Texas Farm Road 2627. This is a couple of miles north of the border of Big Bend National Park. Turn to the southeast on Texas Farm Road 2627. The road cut is 8 miles from your turn.

ROCKHOUNDING

There is a good pullout on the west (right) side. We found a nice variety of colorful agate, jasper, and petrified wood.

84. Terlingua Fossils

Land type: The Edward's Plateau and Hill Country show highly variable vegetation: oak, cedar, mesquite, woodlands, grass prairies, and cypress waterways. This area is more mountainous, there are lots of buttes in the area, and the desert environment is evident. This is mountainous desert.

GPS: 29.2844983 / -103.70236

Elevation: 2,714 feet

Best time of year: All year except when there is snow on the ground

Land manager: Texas Department of Transportation

Material: Marine fossils, calcite

Tools: Geological hammer, small handle rake, screwdriver, spray bottle, garden shovel

Vehicle type: Good road. 2-wheel drive is OK.

Precautions and restrictions: The road can be busy, and the speed limit is high. Be careful pulling off and use your flashers. Snakes are active when the temperature is above 45°F.

Accommodations: Big Bend National Park hosts a number of campsites. Reservations are suggested as it has become a very visited park in recent years. In

Good pull-off here

Sites 84–85

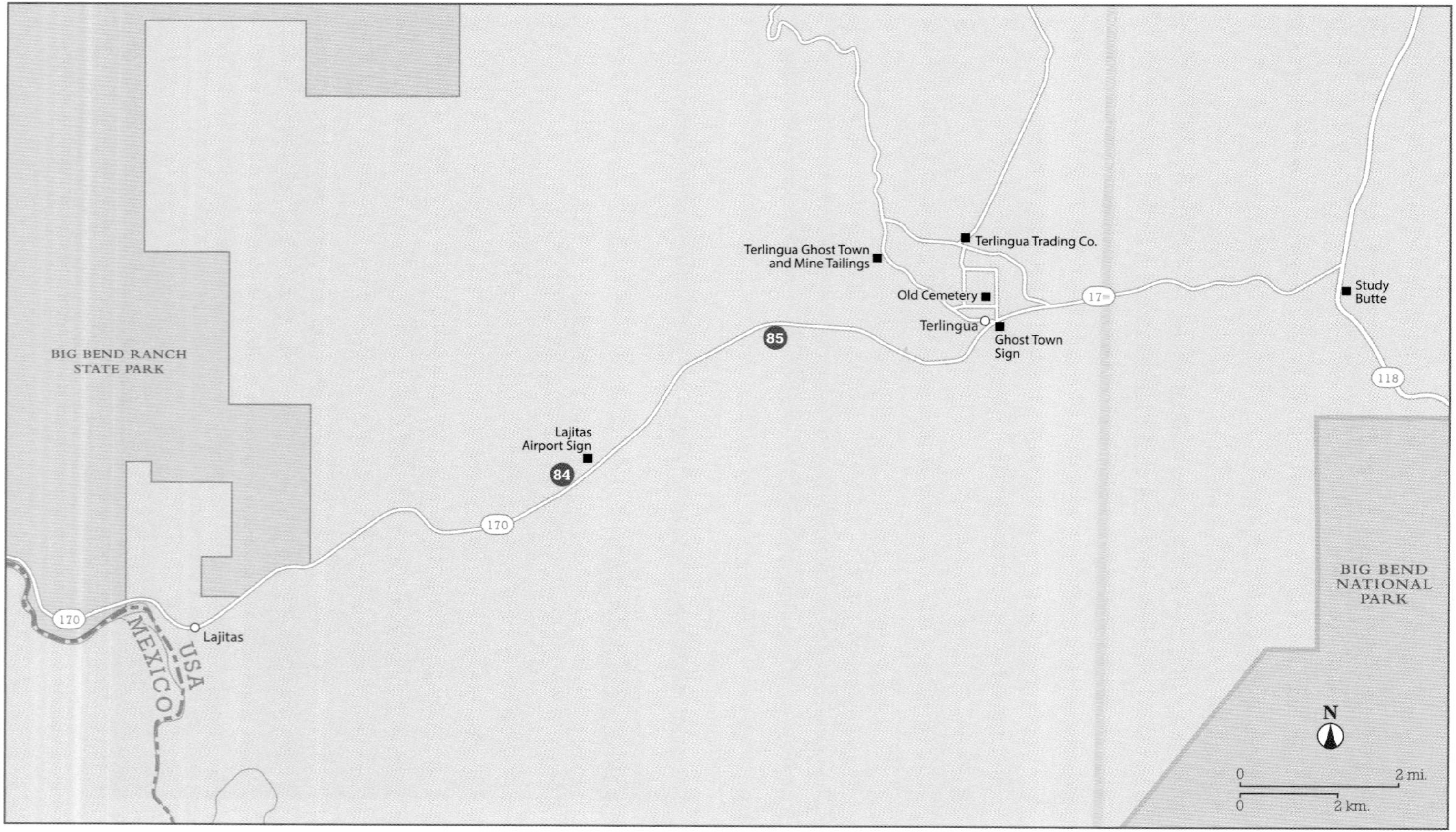

Study Butte

118

Terlingua Trading Co.

Ghost Town Sign

Old Cemetery

Terlingua

Terlingua Ghost Town and Mine Tailings

170

85

Lajitas Airport Sign

84

170

BIG BEND RANCH STATE PARK

BIG BEND NATIONAL PARK

Lajitas

USA

MEXICO

170

N

0   2 km.
0   2 mi.

Typical fossil rock from here

addition, there are a number of private campgrounds in and around Study Butte. Study Butte has a number of motels, hotels, and resorts. There also is a historic hotel within the park.

SPECIAL ATTRACTIONS

Big Bend National Park is well known for hiking trails. These range from very easy to very strenuous. Many folks travel to this park for the great bird watching and wildlife observation. The park boasts a hot pool sitting right on the banks of the Rio Grande River. You can drive to within a quarter mile of the pool. The rangers offer bird-watching tours as well as geology talks. Stargazing is also a very popular activity here because air pollution is very low. The park offers astronomy talks at night.

FINDING THE SITE

Study Butte is a census-designated place in Brewster County and is about 82 miles due south of Alpine, and it takes approximately 1 hour and 21 minutes to drive the distance. This site is about 12 miles west of Study Butte. In Study Butte at the junction of TX 118 and TX 170, turn west onto TX 170 and drive 12.5 miles. There is a large road cut on the south side about 0.1 mile after the Lajitas Airport sign.

ROCKHOUNDING

There isn't a lot here, but with due diligence some nice marine fossils can be found. A screwdriver would be helpful parting the horizontal cleavage of the layered rock. These fossils resemble mussels. We also gathered some nice calcite crystals here.

85. Terlingua Calcite Crystals

See map on page 224.

Land type: The Edward's Plateau and Hill Country show highly variable vegetation: oak, cedar, mesquite, woodlands, grass prairies, and cypress waterways. This area is more mountainous, there are lots of buttes in the area, and the desert environment is evident.

GPS: 29.31898 / -103.6527583

Elevation: 3,234 feet

Best time of year: All year except when there is snow on the ground

Land manager: Texas Department of Transportation

Material: Calcite crystals

Tools: For small pieces: geological hammer, screwdriver, spray bottle, small rake, garden shovel; for larger chunks: sledgehammer, gads, crowbar, chisels, safety glasses, protective gloves, hard hat, and, if you are allergic to dust, a respirator

Vehicle type: Good highway. 2-wheel drive is OK.

Precautions and restrictions: The road can be busy, and the speed limit is high. Be careful pulling off and use your flashers. Snakes are active when the temperature is above 45°F.

The pullout at the calcite location

Accommodations: Big Bend National Park hosts a number of campsites. Reservations are suggested as it has become a very visited park in recent years. In addition, there are a number of private campgrounds in and around Study Butte. Study Butte has a number of motels, hotels, and resorts. There also is a historic hotel within the park.

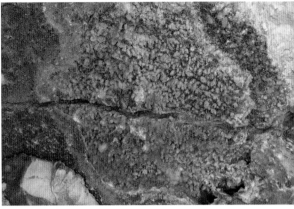
Calcite crystals in the road cut

SPECIAL ATTRACTIONS

Big Bend National Park is well known for hiking trails. These range from very easy to very strenuous. Many folks travel to this park for the great bird watching and wildlife observation. The park boasts a hot pool sitting right on the banks of the Rio Grande River. You can drive to within a quarter mile of the pool. The rangers offer bird-watching tours as well as geology talks. Stargazing is also a very popular activity here because air pollution is very low. The park offers astronomy talks at night.

FINDING THE SITE

Study Butte is a census-designated place in Brewster County and is about 82 miles due south of Alpine, and it takes approximately 1 hour and 21 minutes to drive the distance. This site is west of Study Butte and the Terlingua Ghost Town. In Study Butte at the junction of TX 118 and TX 170, turn west onto TX 170 and drive 7.7 miles. Here you will find a very large road cut.

ROCKHOUNDING

You will see the calcite crystals twinkling on the ground and in the road cut's walls. Lots of nice specimens can be picked up; but to get the best, chiseling on the wall is necessary. This could be dangerous, so make sure you have the proper safety equipment.

86. Study Butte Picture Rock

Land type: The Edward's Plateau and Hill Country show highly variable vegetation: oak, cedar, mesquite, woodlands, grass prairies, and cypress waterways. This area is more mountainous, there are lots of buttes in the area, and the desert environment is evident. This is mountainous desert.

GPS: 29.4393567 / -103.5064033

Elevation: 3,329 feet

Best time of year: All year if there is no snow on the ground

Land manager: Texas Department of Transportation

Material: Picture rock

Tools: For small pieces: geological hammer, screwdriver, spray bottle, small rake, garden shovel; for larger chunks: sledgehammer, gads, crowbar, chisels, safety glasses, protective gloves, hard hat, and, if you are allergic to dust, a respirator

Vehicle type: Good road. 2-wheel drive is sufficient.

Precautions and restrictions: Park well off the road and use your flashers. Watch for snakes if the temperature is 45°F or higher. Be sure to look at the bottom of every rock you pick up. There may be an unwelcome hitchhiker, insect or arachnid,

This is a large area.

Sites 86–93

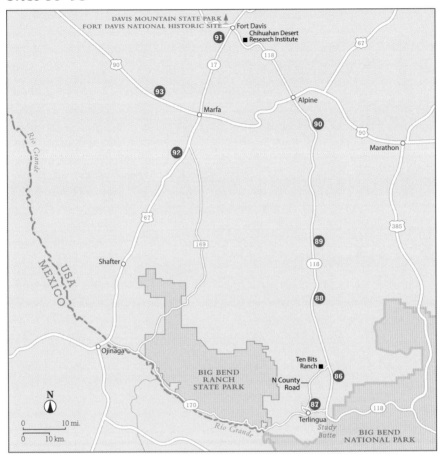

attached and you do not want to rub it or put it in your vehicle. If working for larger pieces, be sure to have all your safety equipment.

Accommodations: Big Bend National Park hosts a number of campsites. Reservations are suggested as it has become a very visited park in recent years. In addition, there are a number of private campgrounds in and around Study Butte. Study Butte has a number of motels, hotels, and resorts. There also is a historic hotel within the park.

SPECIAL ATTRACTIONS

Big Bend National Park is well known for hiking trails. These range from very easy to very strenuous. Many folks travel to this park for the great bird watching

Wonderful patterns in these rocks

and wildlife observation. The park boasts a hot pool sitting right on the banks of the Rio Grande River. You can drive to within a quarter mile of the pool. The rangers offer bird-watching tours as well as geology talks. Stargazing is also a very popular activity here because air pollution is very low. The park offers astronomy talks at night. The area is very touristy. There are a few outfitters around Study Butte as there are kayaking guides and rafting companies.

FINDING THE SITE
Study Butte is a census-designated place in Brewster County and is about 82 miles due south of Alpine, and it takes approximately 1 hour and 21 minutes to drive the distance. From Study Butte at the junction of TX 170 and TX 118, drive north on TX 118 toward Alpine. After 8 miles you will find a road cut on the east side with very high cliffs. Pull off and park.

ROCKHOUNDING
Picture rock comes in at least two different materials. Each hold their own beauty. Some picture rock is composed of rhyolite and others are sandstone. The rhyolite is more colorful and takes a good polish. The sandstone only polishes to a matte finish but really contains the colors of the environment and feel of the desert. The material at this location is sandstone but contains very intricate patterns and shapes. There are lots of small pieces lying around but larger pieces can be obtained by chiseling and prying.

87. North County Road Lavender Rock

Careful here, the road is curvy.

See map on page 229.

Land type: The Edward's Plateau and Hill Country show highly variable vegetation: oak, cedar, mesquite, woodlands, grass prairies, and cypress waterways. This area is more mountainous, there are lots of buttes in the area, and the desert environment is evident. This is mountainous desert.

GPS: 29.4572911 / -103.5599428

Elevation: 3,121 feet

Best time of year: All year except when there is snow on the ground

Land manager: Texas Department of Transportation

Material: Lavender-colored hard rock, dumortierite

Tools: For small pieces: geological hammer, screwdriver, spray bottle, small rake, garden shovel; for larger chunks: sledgehammer, gads, crowbar, chisels, safety glasses, protective gloves, hard hat, and, if you are allergic to dust, a respirator

The color shows up better when polished.

Vehicle type: Good road. 2-wheel drive is OK. There may be occasions, during wet periods, that a 4-wheel drive vehicle would be more appropriate.

Precautions and restrictions: Park well off the road and use your flashers. Watch for snakes if the temperature is 45°F or higher. Be sure to look at the bottom of every rock you pick up. There may be an unwelcome hitchhiker, insect or arachnid, attached and you do not want to rub it or put it in your vehicle.

Accommodations: Big Bend National Park hosts a number of campsites. Reservations are suggested as it has become a very visited park in recent years. In addition, there are a number of private campgrounds in and around Study Butte. Study Butte has a number of motels, hotels, and resorts. There also is a historic hotel within the park.

SPECIAL ATTRACTIONS

Big Bend National Park is well known for hiking trails. These range from very easy to very strenuous. Many folks travel to this park for the great bird watching and wildlife observation. The park boasts a hot pool sitting right on the banks of the Rio Grande River. You can drive to within a quarter mile of the pool. The rangers offer bird-watching tours as well as geology talks. Stargazing is also a very popular activity here because air pollution is very low. The park offers astronomy talks at night.

FINDING THE SITE

Study Butte is a census-designated place in Brewster County, and is about 82 miles due south of Alpine and takes approximately 1 hour and 21 minutes to drive the distance. This site is located about 14 miles from Study Butte. From the junction of TX 170 and TX 118, drive 10.9 miles north on TX 118 to North County Road. Turn west on North County Road and go 3.1 miles to a large rock wall on the left.

ROCKHOUNDING

We're not sure if this is dumortierite or limestone. Dumortierite has a hardness of 7 on the Mohs scale and takes a very good polish, and, therefore if the color is pleasing, makes up into fine cabs for jewelry. It is variably colored aluminium boro-silicate mineral, $Al_7BO_3(SiO_4)_3O_3$, and is fibrous. Dumortierite crystallizes in the orthorhombic system, typically forming fibrous aggregates of slender prismatic crystals. The crystals are orthorhombic, and it is vitreous. The colors vary in color from brown, blue, and green to rarer violet and pink.

We originally drove into this site to search for Hen Egg Mountain agates, geodes, and petrified wood. We did not find any. However, serendipity was with us as we happened upon this pretty lavender material. The rock comes in a number of shades of purple to blue. It takes a good polish and reminds us of dumortierite similar to what was found in southern California. The color is much brighter after the stone is polished.

88. TX 118 Marine Fossils

See map on page 229.
Land type: The Edward's Plateau and Hill Country show highly variable vegetation: oak, cedar, mesquite, woodlands, grass prairies, and cypress waterways. This area is more mountainous, there are lots of buttes in the area, and the desert environment is evident. This is mountainous desert.
GPS: 29.7076097 / -103.5743917
Elevation: 3,991 feet
Best time of year: All year except when there is snow on the ground
Land manager: Texas Department of Transportation
Material: Marine fossils
Tools: Geological hammer, screwdriver, spray bottle, small rake, garden shovel
Vehicle type: Good highway all the way. 2-wheel drive is sufficient.
Precautions and restrictions: Park well off the road and use your flashers. Watch for snakes if the temperature is 45°F or higher. Be sure to look at the bottom of every rock you pick up. There may be an unwelcome hitchhiker, insect or arachnid, attached and you do not want to rub it or put it in your vehicle.

Image of fossil site on TX 118

Image of fossil site on TX 118

Accommodations: Big Bend National Park hosts a number of campsites. Reservations are suggested as it has become a very visited park in recent years. In addition, there are a number of private campgrounds in and around Study Butte. Study Butte has a number of motels, hotels, and resorts. There also is a historic hotel within the park.

SPECIAL ATTRACTIONS

Big Bend National Park is well known for hiking trails. These range from very easy to very strenuous. Many folks travel to this park for the great bird watching and wildlife observation. The park boasts a hot pool sitting right on the banks of the Rio Grande River. You can drive to within a quarter mile of the pool. The rangers offer bird-watching tours as well as geology talks. Stargazing is also a very popular activity here because air pollution is very low. The park offers astronomy talks at night.

FINDING THE SITE

Study Butte is a census-designated place in Brewster County and is about 82 miles due south of Alpine, and it takes approximately 1 hour and 21 minutes to drive the distance. From Study Butte at the intersection of TX 170 and TX 118, head north on TX 118 for 27.5 miles to a very layered road cut.

Typical fossil rock here

Typical fossil rock here

ROCKHOUNDING

We found marine fossil impressions in the layering. These appear to be some sort of mussel. You can wedge pieces off the layered rock with a screwdriver or just walk around picking up random pieces and examining them. The road cut extends for about a quarter of a mile. We did better utilizing the walking around strategy than the wedging-off-of-layers technique.

89. Brewster County Agate

See map on page 229.

Land type: The Edward's Plateau and Hill Country show highly variable vegetation: oak, cedar, mesquite, woodlands, grass prairies, and cypress waterways. This area is more mountainous, there are lots of buttes in the area, and the desert environment is evident. This is mountainous desert.

GPS: 29.8522284 / -103.5769943

Elevation: 2,208 feet

Best time of year: All year except when there is snow on the ground

Land manager: Texas Department of Transportation

Material: Agate, jasper, flint of various colors and patterns

Tools: Geological hammer, garden shovel, short handle rake, spray bottle

Vehicle type: 2-wheel drive is OK. Good road to the site.

Precautions and restrictions: Park well off the road and use your flashers. Watch for snakes if the temperature is 45°F or higher. Be sure to look at the bottom of every rock you pick up. There may be an unwelcome hitchhiker, insect or arachnid, attached and you do not want to rub it or put it in your vehicle.

Lots of tumblers here

Typical assortment of material here

Accommodations: Davis Mountain State Park is about 28 miles northwest of Alpine, and it takes about 35 minutes to drive there. The park offers a variety of camping opportunities. Almost all the sites are very well treed, most with nice views. They offer full hookup, water and electric, water-only, and primitive sites. Besides the state park, there are a lot of commercial campgrounds and RV resorts in Fort Davis and Alpine. Motels and hotels are also available in and near Alpine and Fort Davis.

SPECIAL ATTRACTIONS

Davis Mountain State Park offers many activities for visitors. Bird watching is one of the really popular activities. It is one of the few places where folks can observe Montezuma quail. In fact, the park has a feeding station with a blind set up for observers.

The park boasts some very scenic hiking trails as well as some set up for mountain bikers.

While in the area, a must-visit is the McDonald Observatory. It is located northwest of the town of Fort Davis on Mount Locke. The Frank N. Bash Visitors Center includes a café, gift shop, and interactive exhibit hall. The Visitors Center conducts daily live solar viewings in a large theater, and there are tours of the observatory's largest telescopes. There are also special nights when visitors can look through numerous telescopes of various sizes in the Telescope Park.

In Alpine, rock hounds should not miss seeing the exhibits at the Museum of the Big Bend. These displays depict everything from the natural history of the area, to the human history, to the geology of this part of Texas. It is a must-see.

FINDING THE SITE

Study Butte is a census-designated place in Brewster County and is about 82 miles due south of Alpine, and it takes approximately 1 hour and 21 minutes to drive the distance. From Study Butte at the intersection of TX 170 and TX 118 head north on TX 118 for 37.2 miles. The site is before the "40 miles to Alpine" sign.

ROCKHOUNDING

There are a lot of agates here. However they are quite small but very appropriate for tumbling. With digging around and due diligence, we are sure larger pieces can be located. The agates here are very diverse. Some are clear with interesting inclusions. Others are banded with a great variety of colors. Do not limit yourselves to this particular stop. The entire basin is composed of Lower Cretaceous rock.

90. Alpine Agate and Calcite

See map on page 229.

Land type: The Edward's Plateau and Hill Country show highly variable vegetation: oak, cedar, mesquite, woodlands, grass prairies, and cypress waterways. This area is more mountainous, there are lots of buttes in the area, and the desert environment is evident.

GPS: 30.2555467 / -103.5724967

Elevation: 5,494 feet

Best time of year: All year except when there is snow on the ground

Land manager: Texas Department of Transportation

Material: Agate, calcite

Tools: Geological hammer, short handle rake, garden shovel, spray bottle. If you decide to tackle the vein agate in the wall, you will need gads, chisels, wedge bars, sledgehammer, safety glasses, a respirator if you are sensitive to stone dust, and lots of upper body strength.

Vehicle type: Good road to the site. 2-wheel drive is sufficient.

View of site

Nice specimen from this location

Precautions and restrictions: Park well off the road and use your flashers. Watch for snakes if the temperature is 45°F or higher. Be sure to look at the bottom of every rock you pick up. There may be an unwelcome hitchhiker, insect or arachnid, attached and you do not want to rub it or put it in your vehicle.

Accommodations: Davis Mountain State Park is about 28 miles northwest of Alpine and it takes about 35 minutes to drive there. The park offers a variety of camping opportunities. Almost all the sites are very well treed, most with nice views. They offer full hookup, water and electric, and water-only and primitive sites. Besides the state park, there are a lot of commercial campgrounds and RV resorts in Fort Davis and Alpine. Motels and hotels are also available in and near Alpine and Fort Davis.

SPECIAL ATTRACTIONS

Davis Mountain State Park offers many activities for visitors. Bird watching is one of the really popular activities. It is one of the few places where folks can observe Montezuma quail. In fact, the park has a feeding station with a blind set up for observers.

The park boasts some very scenic hiking trails as well as some set up for mountain bikers.

While in the area, a must-visit is the McDonald Observatory. It is located northwest of the town of Fort Davis on Mount Locke. The Frank N. Bash Visitors Center includes a café, gift shop, and interactive exhibit hall. The Visitors Center conducts daily live solar viewings in a large theater, and there are tours of the observatory's largest telescopes. There are also special nights when visitors can look through numerous telescopes of various sizes in the Telescope Park.

In Alpine, rock hounds should not miss seeing the exhibits at the Museum of the Big Bend. These displays depict everything from the natural history of the area, to the human history, to the geology of this part of Texas. It is a must-see.

FINDING THE SITE

From Alpine at the intersection of US 90 and TX 118, drive south on TX 118 for 12 miles. You will find a big road cut on the east side.

ROCKHOUNDING

This site is a perfect example of how things change. We were last here about 30 years ago and there was a lot of agate and crystalline calcite lying around. This time we picked up only a few small pieces of moss agate. However, it is worth the stop to find the calcite crystals. There is a seam of moss agate running through the rock, but it has been worked at a lot. Perhaps some can still be harvested with a lot of work and muscle using chisels, gads, crowbars, and sledgehammers. If memory serves us, we found a lot of material walking up the sides of the road cut. It is possible to do that and stay on the right-of-way side of the fences. If you are spry enough, you might want to give that a go.

91. Fort Davis Caliche

See map on page 229.

Land type: The Edward's Plateau and Hill Country show highly variable vegetation: oak, cedar, mesquite, woodlands, grass prairies, and cypress waterways. This are is more mountainous, there are lots of buttes in the area, and the desert environment is evident. This is mountainous desert, high desert, and ranch land.

GPS: 30.5579064 / -103.9234286

Elevation: 5,233 feet

Best time of year: All year except when there is snow on the ground. It can be very hot in the summer.

Land manager: Texas Department of Transportation

Material: Caliche

Tools: Geological hammer, short handle rake, garden shovel, spray bottle. If you decide to tackle the vein agate in the wall, you will need gads, chisels, wedge bars, sledgehammer, safety glasses, respirator if you are sensitive to stone dust, and lots of upper body strength.

Look for areas of erosion.

Look for pieces with patterns.

Vehicle type: Good highway to site. 2-wheel drive is sufficient.

Precautions and restrictions: Park well off the road and use your flashers. Watch for snakes if the temperature is 45°F or higher. Be sure to look at the bottom of every rock you pick up. There may be an unwelcome hitchhiker, insect or arachnid, attached and you do not want to rub it or put it in your vehicle.

Accommodations: Davis Mountain State Park is about 15 miles north of this area, and it takes about 20 minutes to drive there. The park offers a variety of camping opportunities. Almost all the sites are very well treed, most with nice views. They offer full hookup, water and electric, and water-only and primitive sites. Besides the state park, there are a lot of commercial campgrounds and RV resorts in Fort Davis and Alpine. Motels and hotels are also available in and near Alpine and Fort Davis.

SPECIAL ATTRACTIONS

Davis Mountain State Park offers many activities for visitors. Bird watching is one of the really popular activities. It is one of the few places where folks can observe Montezuma quail. In fact, the park has a feeding station with a blind set up for observers.

The park boasts some very scenic hiking trail as well as some set up for mountain bikers.

While in the area, a must-visit is the McDonald Observatory. It is located northwest of the town of Fort Davis on Mount Locke. The Frank N. Bash Visitors Center includes a café, gift shop, and interactive exhibit hall. The Visitors Center conducts daily live solar viewings in a large theater, and there are tours of the observatory's largest telescopes. There are also special nights when visitors can look through numerous telescopes of various sizes in the Telescope Park.

In Alpine, rock hounds should not miss seeing the exhibits at the Museum of the Big Bend. These displays depict everything from the natural history of the area, to the human history, to the geology of this part of Texas. It is a must-see.

FINDING THE SITE

From the southern junction of TX 118 and TX 17 in Fort Davis, take TX 17 south for 3.1 miles to a road cut.

ROCKHOUNDING

In Spanish *caliche* means limestone. Indeed, the rock called caliche is a sedimentary rock. It actually is a hardened natural cement of calcium carbonate that binds gravel, sand, clay, and silt. Some deposits are quite fine as opposed to coarse. Some of it is also deposited in different layers. These layers often are of different shades and are very attractive when polished. It produces very pretty bookends and larger jewelry. At this location, collecting is on both sides of the road. Look for the pieces with the most intricate patterns. Pieces up to 3 pounds are quite common. For large specimens you would have to dig and then use chisels, gads, or crowbars to extract them. The deposit goes on for a number of miles on either side of this location. Do not limit yourselves to the location given. Make a number of stops.

92. Marfa Agate Nodules

See map on page 229.
Land type: The Edward's Plateau and Hill Country show highly variable vegetation: oak, cedar, mesquite, woodlands, grass prairies, and cypress waterways. This area is more mountainous, there are lots of buttes in the area, and the desert environment is evident. This is mountainous and hilly desert.
GPS: 30.1730017 / -104.0828567
Elevation: 4,459 feet
Best time of year: Late fall through early spring as long as there is no snow on the ground
Land manager: Texas Department of Transportation
Material: Agate nodules, agate
Tools: Geological hammer, short handle rake, garden shovel, spray bottle. If you decide to tackle the wall, you will need gads, chisels, wedge bars, sledgehammer, safety glasses, respirator if you are sensitive to stone dust, and lots of upper body strength.
Vehicle type: Good road to site. 2-wheel drive is sufficient.

This road cut is full of pockets with nodules.

Precautions and restrictions: Park well off the road and use your flashers. Watch for snakes if the temperature is 45°F or higher. Be sure to look at the bottom of every rock you pick up. There may be an unwelcome hitchhiker, insect or arachnid, attached and you do not want to rub it or put it in your vehicle.

Accommodations: Davis Mountain State Park is about 24 miles northwest of Marfa, and it takes about 25 minutes to drive there. The park offers a variety of camping opportunities. Almost all the sites are very well treed, most with nice views. Besides the state park, there are a lot of commercial campgrounds and RV resorts in Marfa. Motels and hotels are also available in and near Marfa.

SPECIAL ATTRACTIONS

Marfa is a very artsy crafty town. This small desert city in West Texas is known as an arts hub. This town is a place for artists and those who appreciate the arts. Seems like just about every kind of artistic skill is represented. A walk through the town reveals many galleries. You will find paintings, fabrics, photography, and sound and light exhibits. There is a playhouse as well. Marfa sports a number of interesting museums, and there are a number of art festivals each year.

Another popular attraction is the Marfa Lights. This phenomenon is also called the Marfa ghost lights. They are usually observed near US 67 on Mitchell Flat east of Marfa. The real cause of the Marfa Lights is still under debate.

The country rock basalt is full of nodules.

Folks have attributed them to everything from UFOs to ghosts to cattle flatulence and everything you can ever imagine. The state has set up a viewing area for them. However, if you decide to attend the show one evening, you'll be doing so with some very strange folks.

FINDING THE SITE

Marfa is the county seat of Presidio County. It is a small desert town located about 194 miles from El Paso. It takes 2 hours and 55 minutes to drive the distance. From the junction of US 67 and US 90 in downtown Marfa, follow US 67 south for 10.3 miles. Here you will find a large road cut of dark basalt.

ROCKHOUNDING

This was another serendipitous find. About 30 years ago we found a lot of plume agate at a pull-off along this road. It was very abundant, and we had dug probably 5 or 10 pounds of the material to take with us. We used the last of it a number of years ago. It made up into beautiful cabs, which in turn worked up into beautiful jewelry. Well, that said, we could not find the location again—mostly our fault because 30 years ago, we had better memories than we have now and didn't have to write up too many things.

However, even though the plume agate wasn't found, a new discovery was made. As you drive into this pull-off, the white nodules in the basalt will immediately be noticed. They are small but composed of very handsome white, blue, and clear lace agate and quartz crystals. A few might be found on the ground; but for the most part, chiseling, gadding, prying, and hammering are required. It does take a bit of muscle but the effort is worth the results. Take your time and pick the best specimens.

93. Marfa US 90 Agate and Flint

See map on page 229.
Land type: The Edward's Plateau and Hill Country show highly variable
vegetation: oak, cedar, mesquite, woodlands, grass prairies, and cypress
waterways. This area is more mountainous, there are lots of buttes in the area,
and the desert environment is evident. This is ountainous desert and hilly desert
mixed with flat high desert.
GPS: 30.3618921 / -104.1911913
Elevation: 5,070 feet
Best time of year: Late fall through early spring. It can be very hot in the summer.
Land manager: Texas Department of Transportation
Material: Agate, jasper, petrified wood, attractive slag
Tools: Geological hammer, short handle rake, garden shovel, spray bottle
Vehicle type: Good road to the site. 2-wheel drive is sufficient.
Precautions and restrictions: Park well off the road and use your flashers. Watch
for snakes if the temperature is 45°F or higher. Be sure to look at the bottom of

The location is between the road and the railroad track.

Nice agate from this site

every rock you pick up. There may be an unwelcome hitchhiker, insect or arachnid, attached and you do not want to rub it or put it in your vehicle.

Accommodations: Davis Mountain State Park is about 24 miles northwest of Alpine, and it takes about 25 minutes to drive there. The park offers a variety of camping opportunities. Almost all the sites are very well treed, most with nice views. Besides the state park, there are a lot of commercial campgrounds and RV resorts in Marfa. Motels and hotels are also available in and near Marfa.

SPECIAL ATTRACTIONS

Marfa is a very artsy crafty town. It is a small desert city in West Texas, known as an arts hub. This town is the place for artists and those who appreciate the arts. It seems like just about any kind of artistic skill is represented. A walk through the town reveals many galleries. You will find paintings, fabrics, photography, and sound and light exhibits. There is a playhouse as well. Marfa sports a number of interesting museums, and there are a number of art festivals each year.

Another popular attraction is the Marfa Lights. This phenomenon is also called the Marfa ghost lights. They are usually observed near US 67 on Mitchell Flat east of Marfa. While the real cause of the Marfa Lights is still under debate, folks have attributed them to everything from UFOs to ghosts to cattle flatulence and everything you can ever imagine. The state has set up a viewing area for them. However, if you decide to attend the show one evening, you might be doing it with some very strange folks.

FINDING THE SITE

Marfa is the county seat of Presidio County. It is a small desert town located about 194 miles from El Paso. It takes 2 hours and 55 minutes to drive the distance. From the junction of US 67 and US 90 in downtown Marfa, follow US 90 west for 11.2 miles to a flat, open area near the railroad tracks on the right.

ROCKHOUNDING

There is a lot of material here. Some fine petrified wood including palm wood will be noticed immediately. Also found are some really pretty agates in various colors with an assortment of internal patterns and inclusions. Some of the agate was white with a yellow interior. The prize from this location is a clear agate with red inclusions. These make up into fine-looking jewelry pieces. Besides the rocks, some slag, probably from an iron furnace, is present. The material does take a nice polish. It looks like a dark metallic substance when worked on. It was probably used in the rail bed many decades ago. Take a few pieces home. There are quite a few stops like this with plentiful material from Marfa to another 10 miles past this site.

94. Kilbourne Hole

Land type: Desert
GPS: 31.9566666 / -106.9583333
Elevation: 1,292 feet
Best time of year: November through April
Land manager: Bureau of Land Management, Las Cruces District
Material: Peridot, jasper
Tools: Geological hammer
Vehicle type: 4-wheel drive
Precautions and restrictions: This is a very remote area, so make sure that your vehicle is in good shape and you have enough fuel and water. The Border Patrol is usually working in the area, and a lot of locals hunt for rabbits and target shoot here. Be careful of snakes and other poisonous critters.
Accommodations: Franklin Mountains State Park is about 25 miles east of Kilbourne Hole. They offer only primitive camping. Some of the sites are

Image of Kilbourne Hole
NEW MEXICO BUREAU OF GEOLOGY AND MINERAL RESOURCES

Sites 94–95

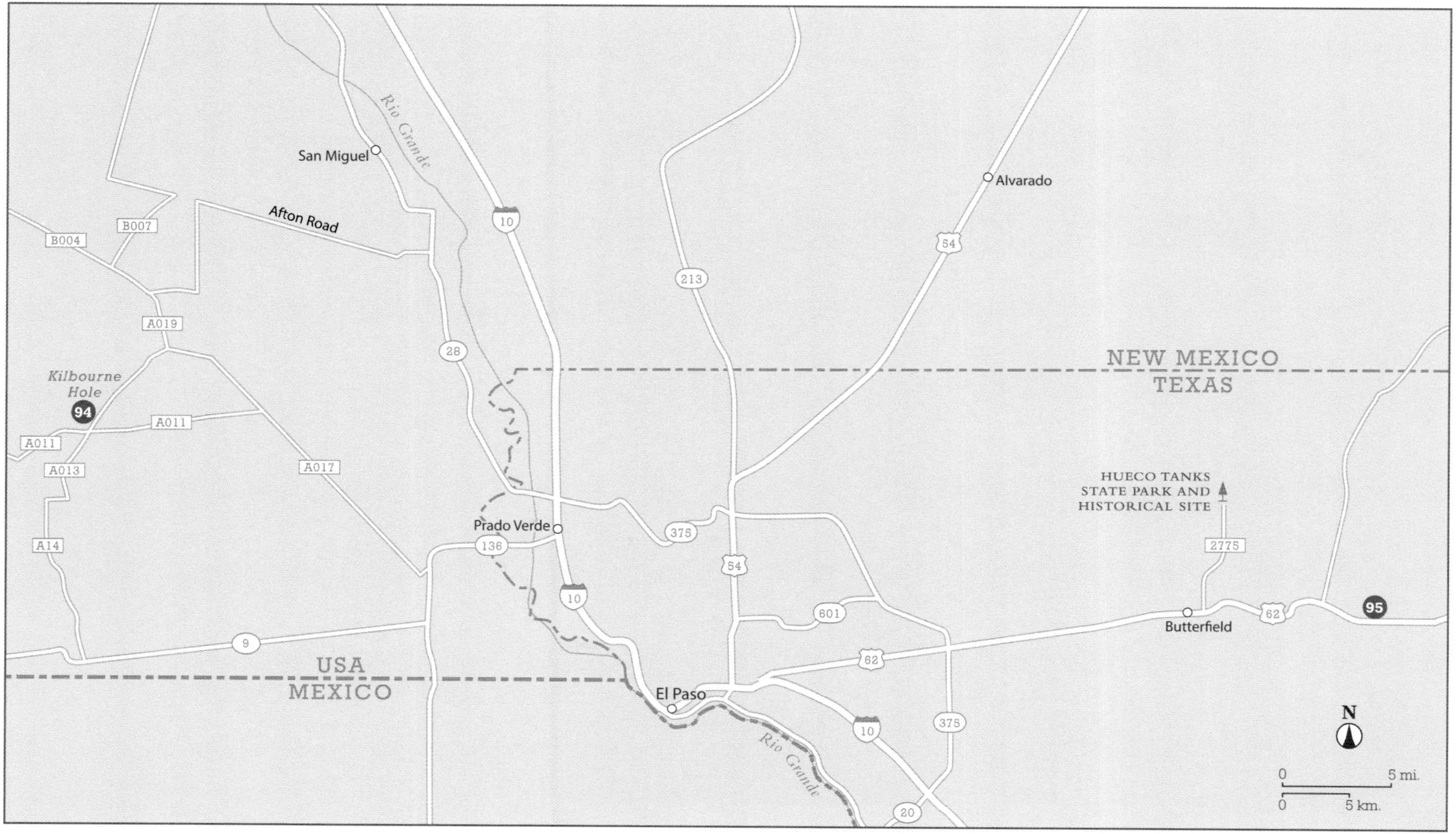

NEW MEXICO
TEXAS

Alvarado

54

213

San Miguel

Rio Grande

Afton Road

28

10

B007

A019

B004

Kilbourne
Hole

94

A011

A013

A017

A14

9

375

54

Prado Verde

10

136

601

82

375

54

El Paso

10

20

375

Rio Grande

HUECO TANKS
STATE PARK AND
HISTORICAL SITE

2275

Butterfield

82

95

USA
MEXICO

N

5 mi.
5 km.
0
0

Kilbourne Hole peridot bomb
NEW MEXICO BUREAU OF GEOLOGY AND MINERAL RESOURCES

walk-in while others can be driven to. All RVs must be self-contained. Private campgrounds and RV resorts abound in the general area. El Paso is a large city, and as such, many motels and hotels are located nearby.

SPECIAL ATTRACTIONS

There are well over 100 miles of hiking trails in Franklin Mountains State Park and a lot more outside the park.

El Paso has a number of municipal parks and a good number of museums. The focus of the various museums include, but are not limited to, history, archeology, art, desert environment, etc.

FINDING THE SITE

This site is actually in New Mexico but is accessed through El Paso, Texas. Kilbourne Hole is located southwest of Las Cruces, New Mexico, and northwest of El Paso, Texas. From exit 11 on I-10, head west on TX 184 (Country Club Road) for 2.6 miles. Turn right (north) onto TX 273 and drive 1.7 miles to a left (west) onto Airport Road. Go 2.5 miles and pass the intersection with TX Highway 136. Continue 0.4 mile and cross railroad tracks. Turn right (northwest) onto an unmarked gravel road paralleling the railroad tracks and drive 1.4 miles. You will cross a cattle guard and then in another 4.8 miles, a second cattle guard. Go straight for another 4.3 miles, where yet another cattle guard will be crossed. After another 0.4 mile make a left (west) onto CR A011. After 4.1 miles you will cross a desert road. Continue another 3.9 miles, passing a green water tank on the left (north) side, to Kilbourne Hole.

ROCKHOUNDING

This site boasts some very gemmy peridot. The stones were formed when a volcano erupted about 80,000 years ago. They come in the form of "bombs," which are plain brown on the outside. When chopped open, the clear green gems are obvious.

When you get to the crater, climb up the rim and then down into the hole. The bombs are rather difficult to spot, as they look like most of the other rocks. Once you figure it out, though, they will become apparent.

Most of the peridot grains inside the bombs are too small to do much with. We mixed a bunch of them with epoxy and then polished the conglomerate like a cab. The result was quite pretty. Some of the bombs hold coarse grains, and it's possible to find pieces that could be faceted into 1/4- to 1/2-carat gems, though these are very scarce.

Who knows? You may find the bomb that has 1- or 2-carat stones inside. Good luck!

95. Hueco Tanks Flint, Agate, and Jasper

See map on page 253.

Land type: Desert mountains and basins. Vegetation includes ocotillo, mountain pines, junipers, yucca, and ponderosa pines.

GPS: 31.82752 / -105.91913

Elevation: 4,520 feet

Best time of year: All year. It can be very hot in summer.

Land manager: Texas Department of Transportation

Material: Flint, agate

Tools: For small pieces: geological hammer, short handle rake, garden shovel, and spray bottle; for large chunks: gads, chisels, crow bar, and sledgehammer

Vehicle type: Good road all the way to the site. 2-wheel drive is sufficient.

Precautions and restrictions: Be sure to pull completely off the pavement. Use your warning flashers. This road is narrow in places and pulling off the pavement can be difficult. Snakes and venomous insects are in the area. Use a snake stick when near brush. Examine every rock you keep for unwanted hitchhikers.

Agate and flint from Hueco Tanks road location

Accommodations: Hueco Tanks State Park is within a few miles of this location. They offer sites with electricity and water or water-only parking. Due to the sensitive environment, this park is not very dog friendly. All pets must be on leash and can only be walked on paved paths. They cannot be left in the vehicle alone. Leaving Rover with some friends is a better option if you intend to spend time here.

SPECIAL ATTRACTIONS

The park offers rock climbing, bird watching, hiking, nature and history study, and stargazing. Guided and self-guided tours to view rock imagery are available.

FINDING THE SITE

Starting in El Paso, take US 62/180 east. After you pass the access road to Hueco Tanks State Park, Texas Farm Road 2775, drive another 9 miles. This is where the GPS numbers were taken. The collecting area continues for a number of miles farther on.

ROCKHOUNDING

In the past, it was possible to find large pieces of flint and agate in this area. They are still there, but you have to look a little harder. There still are lots of tumbler-size pieces lying around. Do not limit yourself to this location. Keep driving and pull off wherever you can. More material will be found.

96. Toyah Agate and Petrified Wood

Land type: Desert mountains and basins are mixed with flat ranch land. Dominant plants include ocotillo, yucca, junipers, mountain pines, and ponderosa pines.
GPS: 31.3130263 / -103.8129741
Elevation: 2,997 feet
Best time of year: Late fall through early spring except when there is snow on the ground. It can be very hot in the summer.
Land manager: Texas Department of Transportation

The Toyah agate location

Material: Agate, flint, jasper, petrified wood
Tools: Geological hammer, short handle rake, garden shovel, spray bottle
Vehicle type: Good road. Paved until the last mile or two, but the gravel appears to be well maintained. 2-wheel drive is sufficient.
Precautions and restrictions: Finding a pull-off could be challenging here. Keep driving until you see a good parking area. The road is narrow in spots. Use your warning flashers when parked. This is prime rattlesnake territory. They are active when the temperature is higher than 45°F. Make lots of noise and use snake sticks.
Accommodations: Balmorhea State Park is about 29 miles from Kent. It takes around a half hour to drive there. The campground offers sites with full hookups or ones with just electric and water. At the time of this writing, the camping area of the park was closed due to renovations. However, it should reopen soon. There are some private RV camps and resorts around Toyah and Van Horn as well as motels and hotels.

Sites 96–99

Most of the agate and petrified wood from this location are in light muted colors.

SPECIAL ATTRACTIONS

Balmorhea State Park is quite unique. It boasts a warm water pool where the water is drawn from the San Solomon Springs, which is a natural spring with temperatures between 72 and 76°F. The pool holds 3.5 million gallons of water, is 25 feet deep, and covers 1.3 acres. Visitors to the park can swim, and scuba diving is available. Scuba diving instruction is given by certified instructors for an additional fee.

Balmorhea blue is a famous form of agate that is found in the hills behind the state park. However, the source has been depleted for many years so we did not put it in this book as a location. Occasionally, some folks do find a piece or two. You may be one of the lucky ones. So give it a try.

FINDING THE SITE

From I-10, take the only exit into the town of Toyah. You will come out on South Center Street; turn north onto South Center Street. Soon after crossing the railroad tracks, South Center Street ends at North Front Street. Turn right on North Front Street and take the first left on DuBois Street. Drive north 4 blocks on DuBois Street to N 4th Street. Turn left onto N 4th Street and drive 1.4 miles just past the junction of CR 232.

ROCKHOUNDING

This site is surrounded by agate-producing hills and mountains. The gravels are washed down from the heights and deposited in the basin. This location used to be very prolific. Agate of every description and color has been picked up here. The prize find here was a deep blue plume agate. Many years ago we had found some of this with red swirls mixed in.

Over the years, this site has been picked over. However, it holds enough nice material to make a stop worthwhile. Recently, we stopped for about an hour and collected a dozen nice pieces. That wasn't too bad except for our memories of what used to be here. Do not limit yourselves to the GPS numbers we list. The area goes on for miles. Perhaps you will find a piece of that deep blue.

97. Garden City Agate and Flint

See map on page 259.

Land type: The Edward's Plateau and Hill Country show highly variable vegetation: oak, cedar, mesquite, woodlands, grass prairies, and cypress waterways.

GPS: 31.8284502 / 101310071

Elevation: 2,625 feet

Best time of year: Late fall through early spring except when there is snow on the ground. **It c**an be very hot in the summer.

Land manager: Texas Department of Transportation

Material: Agate, flint, jasper, petrified wood

Tools: Geological hammer, short handle rake, garden shovel, and spray bottle if you only intend to pick up what is on the ground. If you decide to tackle the vein agate in the wall, you will need gads, chisels, wedge bars, sledgehammer, safety glasses, respirator if you are sensitive to stone dust, and lots of upper body strength.

Vehicle type: Good highway all the way to the site. 2-wheel drive is sufficient.

The location near Garden City

Some of the material here is translucent and makes fine cabs and tumblers.

Precautions and restrictions: Park well off the road and use your flashers. Watch for snakes if the temperature is 45°F or higher. Be sure to look at the bottom of every rock you pick up. There may be an unwelcome hitchhiker, insect or arachnid, attached and you do not want to rub it or put it in your vehicle.

Accommodations: Garden City is about 75 miles northwest of San Angelo State Park. It takes a little more than an hour to drive the distance. This park offers a variety of camping opportunities. They offer about 80 sites with water and electricity and about 10 sites with just water. In addition, there are about 10 primitive campsites at this park.

SPECIAL ATTRACTIONS

Fishing in O.C. Fisher Reservoir or the Concho River is good. The state park is located on the shores of these waterways. You don't need a fishing license to fish from shore or pier in a state park.

Nature and bird watching are popular activities at Big Spring State Park. There is a paved 3-mile hiking and biking trail to be enjoyed.

FINDING THE SITE

Garden City is an unincorporated community and census-designated place in Glasscock County. It is south of Midland and about 290 miles southwest of

Fort Worth. It takes about 4 hours to drive from Fort Worth to Garden City. From Garden City at the junction of Texas Farm Road 33 and TX 158, travel southeast on TX 158 for 8.8 miles to a very large road cut on both sides. There are very big parking areas extending about 1/8th of a mile.

ROCKHOUNDING

There is a lot of very colorful flint and agate both on the ground and still attached to the walls of the road cut. You can pick up pieces off the ground, or with great effort using gads, chisels, sledgehammers, and crowbars extract pieces from the wall. The material on the ground is probably tailings from others engaged in this activity. You will see both nodules and seams of agate. As far as color and patterns, the seam flint and nodules are very closely related.

98. Sterling City Flint, Agate, and Patterned Rhyolite

See map on page 259.

Land type: The Edward's Plateau and Hill Country show highly variable vegetation: oak, cedar, mesquite, woodlands, grass prairies, and cypress waterways.

GPS: 31.8291986 / -101.1847968

Elevation: 2,556 feet

Best time of year: Late fall through early spring except when there is snow on the ground. **It c**an be very hot in the summer.

Land manager: Texas Department of Transportation

Material: Agate, flint, rhyolite

Tools: Geological hammer, short handle rake, garden shovel, spray bottle

Vehicle type: Good highway all the way to the site. 2-wheel drive is sufficient.

Precautions and restrictions: Park well off the road and use your flashers. It is quite grassy at the margins of the right-of-way. Watch for snakes if the temperature is 45°F or higher. Be sure to look at the bottom of every rock you

Sterling City location

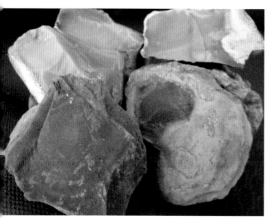
Some of the material here is very similar to that at Garden City.

pick up. There may be an unwelcome hitchhiker, insect or arachnid, attached and you do not want to rub it or put it in your vehicle.

Accommodations: Sterling City is about 45 miles northwest of San Angelo State Park. It takes a little more than an hour to drive the distance. This park offers a variety of camping opportunities. They offer about 80 sites with water and electricity and about 10 sites with just water. In addition, there are about 10 primitive campsites.

SPECIAL ATTRACTIONS

Fishing in O.C. Fisher Reservoir or the Concho River is good. The state park is located on the shores of these waterways. You don't need a fishing license to fish from shore or pier in a state park.

Nature and bird watching are popular activities at Big Spring State Park. There is a paved 3-mile hiking and biking trail to be enjoyed.

FINDING THE SITE

Sterling City is the county seat of Sterling County. It is about 250 miles southeast of Fort Worth with a drive time of 3 hours and 45 minutes. If you are coming from Sterling City, a few miles west is the junction of TX 158 and US 87; drive northwest on TX 158 for 9.4 miles.

If coming from Garden City, from the junction of Texas Farm Road 33 and TX 158, drive southeast on TX 158 for 19.2 miles. You will see a small road cut on the right side.

ROCKHOUNDING

Here the material is rather difficult to recognize until it is chipped, then the beautiful colors and patterns will be seen. Besides the agate and flint, you will find a very pretty rhyolite among the mix. This material is very similar to that found at the previous Site 97, Garden City Agate and Flint. The difference is that the material at the previous site has just recently been exposed by human excavation. The material here had eroded out of the strata many eons ago.

99. South of Colorado City Flint and Agate

See map on page 259.
Land type: The Edward's Plateau and Hill Country show highly variable vegetation: oak, cedar, mesquite, woodlands, grass prairies, and cypress waterways. This is rolling ranch land and desert.
GPS: 32.1848452 / -101.0147288
Elevation: 2,165 feet
Best time of year: Late fall through early spring except when there is snow on the ground. **It c**an be very hot in the summer.
Land manager: Texas Department of Transportation
Material: Agate, flint
Tools: Geological hammer, short handle rack, garden shovel, spray bottle
Vehicle type: Good highway all the way to the site. 2-wheel drive is sufficient.
Precautions and restrictions: Park well off the road and use your flashers. It is quite grassy at the margins of the right-of-way. Watch for snakes if the temperature is 45°F or higher.

The pull-off south of Colorado City

Accommodations: Colorado City is about 80 miles north-northwest of San Angelo State Park. It takes a little more than 1 hour and 15 minutes to drive the distance. This park offers a variety of camping opportunities. They offer about 80 sites with water and electricity and about 10 sites with just water. In addition, there are about 10 primitive campsites at the park.

SPECIAL ATTRACTIONS

Fishing in O.C. Fisher Reservoir or the Concho River is good. The state park is located on the shores of these waterways. You don't need a fishing license to fish from shore or pier in a state park.

Nature and bird watching are popular activities at Big Spring State Park. There is a paved 3-mile hiking and biking trail to be enjoyed.

FINDING THE SITE

Colorado City is a city in and the county seat of Mitchell County. It is about 220 miles from Fort Worth with a drive time of about 3 hours and 10 minutes. From Colorado City at the junction of TX 163 and Business I-20, which is also called West 2nd Street, drive south on TX 163 for 17.6 miles.

If traveling from near Sterling City, at the junction of US 87 and TX 163 drive north for 22.8 miles on TX 163.

ROCKHOUNDING

The shoulder of the road adjacent to the collecting site slopes down rather severely. A flatter area is located about a hundred yards to the north. Park here and walk back. There is a lot of material at this site. We found agate, flint, and nice petrified wood.

THE PANHANDLE

A number of guidebooks and websites claim that the Panhandle region, while offering some opportunities, is not the most prolific area of Texas to rock-hound in. We think they are wrong. This area has some of the nicest flint available in Texas. In addition, for those interested in carving, there are a good number of alabaster sites available for the rock hound.

Lower Cretaceous fossils are abundant in some areas; and the petrified wood is very diverse and well agatized, some is even opalized. There have been reports of geodes found around the canyonlands, so that, too, is a possibility.

As far as we can determine, because the Panhandle is so agricultural, there are few if any opportunities to collect on private land. Again, this changes over time so it may be advantageous to check the status of this type of rockhound-ing if you enjoy that kind of collecting.

Weather can be a problem in the Panhandle. The temperatures can be unbearably hot in the summer and very cold in the winter. Big winds are quite common as are storms and the occasional tornado. The most serious condition here is the variability of the weather, its unpredictability, and swift-ness of change. A beautiful day can turn into a maelstrom in very short order. What we're saying is be prepared for just about any kind of meteorological event. Many enjoy the autumn to collect here because the temperature has moderated and the snake population becomes less active and heads toward their winter hibernation headquarters.

100. Justiceburg Marine Fossils

Land type: Rolling plains, mesquite, woodland, and grass prairie
GPS: 32.9811633 / -101.1112283
Elevation: 2,385 feet
Best time of year: Any time there is no snow on the ground
Land manager: Texas Department of Transportation
Material: Marine fossils, flint
Tools: Geological hammer, short handle rake, garden shovel, spray bottle
Vehicle type: Good highway all the way to the site. 2-wheel drive is sufficient.
Precautions and restrictions: Park well off the road and use your flashers. It is quite grassy at the margins of the right-of-way. Watch for snakes if the temperature is 45°F or higher.
Accommodations: Post is about a hundred miles south of Caprock Canyon State Park, and it takes about an hour and a half to drive the distance. The park offers a variety of camping opportunities. They have sites with 30- or 50-amp electric service and water, and water-only sites.

The Justiceburg fossil location

Sites 100–108

Nicely preserved fossils from Justiceburg

SPECIAL ATTRACTIONS

Caprock State Park and Trailway is a wonderful diversion for rock hounds. The rock formations are fascinating, and there is a very diverse assortment of hiking trails. A favorite is the Caprock Trailway. This hiking trail meanders through much of Caprock Escarpment. It begins in the east in the Red River valley and terminates in the west at South Plains on top of the Caprock Escarpment. It crosses forty-six bridges and passes through three counties (Floyd, Briscoe, and Hall). The railway is about 65 miles for those who want the challenge of a multi-night adventure. However, it is broken up into 5- to 12-mile segments for those who just want a short day experience. This is one of the Panhandle's premier attractions.

FINDING THE SITE

Post is a city in Garza County. It is about 40 miles southeast of Lubbock, and it takes about 38 minutes to drive there. From the town of Post at the junction of US 84 and the south end of Texas Loop Road Avenue F, drive south on US 84 for 20.8 miles to an open road cut on both sides. Parking off the road is easier on the east side. The site is just south of the small town of Justiceburg.

ROCKHOUNDING

We made a random stop here and to our delight the soil was full of loose fossils. These included gastropods, brachiopods, bivalves, and crinoid stems. Don't limit yourselves to this location. There will be fossils almost anywhere you stop within a few miles.

101. Turkey Alabaster

Look for the light-colored areas.

See map on page 271.
Land type: Rolling plains
GPS: 34.4257135 / -100.909721
Elevation: 2,525.9 feet
Best time of year: All year except when snow is present
Land manager: Texas Department of Transportation
Material: Alabaster for carving
Tools: Geological hammer, short handle rake, garden shovel, and spray bottle.
If large pieces are desired, a sledgehammer, gads, crowbar, and chisel would be needed along with lots of upper body strength.
Vehicle type: Good highway. 2-wheel drive is fine.
Precautions and restrictions: A little tight parking. Pull off the pavement and use flashers.
Accommodations: Turkey is about 15 miles southeast of Caprock Canyon State Park, and it takes about 20 minutes to drive the distance. The park offers a variety of camping opportunities. They have sites with 30- or 50-amp electric service and water, and water-only sites.

SPECIAL ATTRACTIONS

Caprock State Park and Trailway is a wonderful diversion for rock hounds. The rock formations are fascinating, and there is a very diverse assortment of hiking trails. A favorite is the Caprock Trailway. This hiking trail meanders through much of Caprock Escarpment. It begins in the east in the Red River valley and terminates in the west at South Plains on top of the Caprock Escarpment. It crosses forty-six bridges and passes through three counties (Floyd, Briscoe, and Hall). The railway is about 65 miles for those who want the challenge of a multi-night adventure. However, it is broken up into 5- to 12-mile segments for those who just want a short day experience. This is one of the Panhandle's premier attractions.

FINDING THE SITE

Turkey is a small city in Hall County. It is about 100 miles southeast of Amarillo with a drive time of about an hour and a half. From the junction of TX 86 and TX 70 in the town of Turkey, drive north on TX 86/70 for 0.7 mile where the roads separate. Bear to the left on TX 70 for 1.8 miles to the road cut.

ROCKHOUNDING

Alabaster is a fine-grained form of gypsum and is usually translucent. The chemical makeup of this rock is hydrated calcium sulfate. It is mainly within sedimentary deposits and can be used to make plaster of Paris and fertilizers. While the color is often white, it is often slightly tinted with other colors such as green, pink, orange, or even blue. This material is very soft, 1 to 2 on the Mohs scale, and suitable for carving. At this site the material is variated rose and grey. Small pieces were everywhere, but for sizable chunks a lot of muscle and hard work are required.

Turkey alabaster

102. Quitaque Alabaster

Quitaque Alabaster site

See map on page 271.
Land type: Rolling plains, river breaks, and canyons
GPS: 34.3777367 / -101.1072117
Elevation: 2,852 feet
Best time of year: Any time there is no snow on the ground
Land manager: Texas Department of Transportation
Material: Alabaster
Tools: Geological hammer, short handle rake, garden shovel, and spray bottle.
If large pieces are desired, a sledgehammer, gads, crowbar, and chisel would be
needed along with lots of upper body strength.
Vehicle type: Good highway. 2-wheel drive is fine.
Precautions and restrictions: Be sure to pull completely off the pavement. The
road is a bit narrow here. Use your warning flashers. Think about snakes when the
temperature is higher than 45°F.

Accommodations: Quitaque is about 6 miles south of Caprock Canyon State Park, and it takes about 15 minutes to drive the distance. The park offers a variety of camping opportunities. They have sites with 30-or 50-amp electric service and water, and water-only sites.

SPECIAL ATTRACTIONS

Caprock State Park and Trailway is a wonderful diversion for rock hounds. The rock formations are fascinating, and there is a very diverse assortment of hiking trails. A favorite is the Caprock Trailway. This hiking trail meanders through much of Caprock Escarpment. It begins in the east in the Red River valley and terminates in the west at South Plains on top of the Caprock Escarpment. It crosses forty-six bridges and passes through three counties (Floyd, Briscoe, and Hall). The railway is about 65 miles for those who want the challenge of a multi-night adventure. However, it is broken up into 5- to 12-mile segments for those who just want a short day experience. This is one of the Panhandle's premier attractions.

FINDING THE SITE

Quitaque is a city in southeastern Briscoe County. It is about 95 miles southeast of Amarillo, and it takes about an hour and a half to drive the distance. From the junction of TX 86 and Texas Farm Road 1065 in the town of Quitaque, drive 3 miles west on TX 86 to a rocky road cut.

ROCKHOUNDING

Alabaster is a fine-grained form of gypsum and is usually translucent. The chemical makeup of this rock is hydrated calcium sulfate. It is mainly within sedimentary deposits and can be used to make plaster of Paris and fertilizers. While the color is often white, it is often slightly tinted with other colors such as green, pink, orange, or even blue. This material is very soft, 1 to 2 on the Mohs scale, and suitable for carving. At this site the material is variated rose and grey. Small pieces are everywhere, but for sizable chunks a lot of muscle and hard work are required. Big pieces can be extracted from this site.

103. MacKenzie Lake

Mackenzie Lake site

See map on page 271.
Land type: High rolling plains, hills, and canyons
GPS: 34.5499117 / -101.4379133
Elevation: 3,234 feet
Best time of year: Spring, summer, fall
Land manager: MacKenzie Municipal Water Authority
Material: Petrified wood, gypsum crystals
Tools: Geological hammer, short handle rake, garden shovel, and spray bottle for the petrified wood. If you are after gypsum crystals, a sledgehammer, gads, crowbar, and chisel would be needed. Also, have a good supply of soft tissue paper. This will be needed to transport the delicate crystals home.
Vehicle type: Good road all the way to the site. 2-wheel drive is sufficient.
Precautions and restrictions: This property is administrated by the MacKenzie Municipal Water Authority. Be sure to pay the fees required and carry a receipt on your person.

Small pieces of alabaster from this area

Accommodations: You can camp right at the site. The MacKenzie Municipal Water Authority runs a lovely campground right on the property. There are a number RV campsites. They are rented on a per night basis. Water and 50-amp electric connections are provided at each campsite. Dump stations are located on the property. In addition to the camping opportunities, the Authority has two vacation rental cabins available.

SPECIAL ATTRACTIONS

Fishing in Mackenzie Lake is quite good. It is a low-pressure body of water so if you like to fish alone, this is a good place to pursue your sport. Largemouth bass is the species that most folks pursue. The lake has good numbers between 2 and 4 pounds. Crappie are also abundant as are blue catfish. If you'd like to pursue hybrid striped bass, fish the open lake around drop-offs.

The lake also sports a number of hiking trails. For the motorsport enthusiast, there are some ATV trails.

FINDING THE SITE

Silverton is a city in Briscoe County. It is about 79 miles southeast of Amarillo, and it takes about 1 hour and 15 minutes to drive the distance. The lake is located northwest of the town of Silverton. At the junction of TX 207 and TX 86, drive northwest on TX 207 for 6.9 miles to the gated entrance on the left to the MacKenzie Lake area.

ROCKHOUNDING

Entrance to this area requires a fee. There are a number of areas around the lake where the collecting of selenite and petrified wood is good. You will note sparkling in the hills. These are gypsum crystals. If you intend to collect these, be prepared. They are very fragile and require special handling. Have lots of soft tissue paper available to wrap them for the trip home. Alabaster is also a common find around the lake.

104. Near Clarendon Ogallala Gravels

A site of the Ogallala gravel exposure

See map on page 271.
Land type: Rolling plains and grassy hills and farmland
GPS: 34.8275777 / -100.8838239
Elevation: 2,892 feet
Best time of year: Spring, summer, and fall
Land manager: Texas Department of Transportation
Material: Agatized wood, opalized wood, feldspar, manganese nodules, colorful quartzite pebbles
Tools: Geological hammer, short handle rake, garden shovel, and spray bottle for the petrified wood
Vehicle type: Good road all the way to the site. 2-wheel drive is sufficient.
Precautions and restrictions: Be sure to pull completely off the pavement. The road is a bit narrow here. Use your warning flashers. Watch for snakes when the temperature is over 45°F.

Quartzite and flint from this site

Accommodations: Claredon is about 58 miles south of Caprock Canyon State Park, and it takes a little more than an hour to drive the distance. The park offers a variety of camping opportunities. They have sites with 30- or 50-amp electric service and water, and water-only sites. There are motels and some commercial RV parks in and around Clarendon.

SPECIAL ATTRACTIONS

Caprock State Park and Trailway is a wonderful diversion for rock hounds. The rock formations are fascinating, and there is a very diverse assortment of hiking trails. A favorite is the Caprock Trailway. This hiking trail meanders through much of Caprock Escarpment. It begins in the east in the Red River valley and terminates in the west at South Plains on top of the Caprock Escarpment. It crosses forty-six bridges and passes through three counties (Floyd, Briscoe, and Hall). The railway is about 65 miles for those who want the challenge of a multi-night adventure. However, it is broken up into 5- to 12-mile segments for those who just want a short day experience. This is one of the Panhandle's premier attractions.

FINDING THE SITE

Clarendon is a city in Donley County. It is located about 60 miles southeast of Amarillo, and it takes a little less than an hour to drive the distance. From the town at the junction of TX 70 and US 287, travel south on TX 70 for 7.5 miles.

ROCKHOUNDING

A mix of highly colorful quartzite pebbles, agatized wood and feldspar, opalized wood, and the occasional hollowed out manganese nodules can be found here. We did not find any of the opalized wood or manganese nodules. But, then again, that doesn't mean you won't.

105. Memphis Quartzite and Flint

Roadside location of the Memphis quartzite location

See map on page 271.
Land type: High rolling hills and canyons
GPS: 34.7242367 / -100.3795917. These were taken a few hundred yards up the hill because there was no signal directly at the site.
Elevation: 2,057 feet
Best time of year: Spring, summer, fall
Land manager: Texas Department of Transportation
Material: Quartzite, flint
Tools: Geological hammer, short handle rake, garden shovel, spray bottle
Vehicle type: Good road all the way to the site. 2-wheel drive is sufficient.
Precautions and restrictions: Be sure to pull completely off the pavement. The road is a bit narrow here. Use your warning flashers.
Accommodations: Memphis is about 53 miles northeast of Caprock Canyon State Park, and it takes a little less than an hour to drive the distance. The park offers a variety of camping opportunities. They have sites with 30- or 50-amp electric

service and water, water-only RV sites, and walk-in tent sites. There are motels and some commercial RV parks in and around Memphis and Wellington.

SPECIAL ATTRACTIONS

Caprock State Park and Trailway is a wonderful diversion for rock hounds. The rock formations are fascinating, and there is a very diverse assortment of hiking trails. A favorite is the Caprock Trailway. This hiking trail meanders through much of Caprock Escarpment. It begins in the east in the Red River valley and terminates in the west at South Plains on top of the Caprock Escarpment. It crosses forty-six bridges and passes through three counties (Floyd, Briscoe, and Hall). The railway is about 65 miles for those who want the challenge of a multi-night adventure. However, it is broken up into 5- to 12-mile segments for those who just want a short day experience. This is one of the Panhandle's premier attractions.

FINDING THE SITE

Memphis is a city in and the county seat of Hall County. It is about 86 miles southeast of Amarillo with a drive time of about 1 hour and 15 minutes. From Memphis at the junction of US 287 and TX 256, drive east on TX 256 for 7.2 miles to the road cut. If you are coming from the other direction, from Wellington at the junction of 15th Street and US 83, drive south on US 83 for 11.3 miles to the junction of US 83 and TX 256. Turn west and drive toward Memphis on TX 256 for 12.8 miles to the road cut.

Assortment of quartzite and flint from this location

ROCKHOUNDING

You will notice high banks of very red soil on both sides of the road. Some very colorful pebbles of quartzite can be picked up here. They range in color from red, yellow, green, blue, and mixtures of all of the above. These take a high polish and tumble really well. Some larger pebbles are big enough for slicing. You will also find an occasional piece of flint.

106. Childress Banded Limestone and Quartzite

Pull-off at the Childress site

See map on page 271.
Land type: Rolling plain with mesquite, woodlands, and grass prairies
GPS: 34.5884183 / -100.18923
Elevation: 1,870 feet
Best time of year: Spring, summer, fall
Land manager: Texas Department of Transportation
Material: Quartzite, banded limestone
Tools: Geological hammer, short handle rake, garden shovel, and spray bottle for the petrified wood. If you are after gypsum crystals, a sledgehammer, gads, crowbar, and chisel would be needed.
Vehicle type: Good road all the way to the site. 2-wheel drive is sufficient.
Precautions and restrictions: Be sure to pull completely off the pavement. The road is a bit narrow here. Use your warning flashers.
Accommodations: The City of Childress runs an RV park at the Childress City Fair Park. They have a number of sites with water and 30- or 50-amp electric service.

Material from this location

It is a simple overnight spot that is relatively inexpensive at the time of this writing. It's basically just a parking lot with some hookups.

SPECIAL ATTRACTIONS
The Childress City Fair Park has a lake for fishing. A very pretty trail runs around the perimeter of the lake. It is a great place for bird watching and getting a little exercise.

Caprock State Park and Trailway is about 62 miles east of Childress. It takes a little bit more than an hour to drive the distance. This park is a wonderful diversion for rock hounds. The rock formations are fascinating, and there is a very diverse assortment of hiking trails. A favorite is the Caprock Trailway. This hiking trail meanders through much of Caprock Escarpment. It begins in the east in the Red River valley and terminates in the west at South Plains on top of the Caprock Escarpment. It crosses forty-six bridges and passes through three counties (Floyd, Briscoe, and Hall). The railway is about 65 miles for those who want the challenge of a multi-night adventure. However, it is broken up into 5- to 12-mile segments for those who just want a short day experience. This is one of the Panhandle's premier attractions.

FINDING THE SITE
Childress is a city in Childress County, and it is the county seat. The city is 117 miles southeast of Amarillo with a drive time of about 1 hour and 45 minutes. From the town of Childress at the junction of US 62/83 and US 287, travel north on US 62/83 to a grassy road cut on both sides.

ROCKHOUNDING
This was another random stop. And we were pleasantly surprised. There were lovely banded limestone pieces littering the ground. Larger pieces can be had by chiseling and gadding. These would make fine larger items such as bookends. The smaller pieces can be used as tumblers and even handsome cabs.

Besides the limestone, we picked up colorful quartzite pebbles. These also would make fine tumbling material. Some of the pebbles were large enough to slice and be cabbed into nice jewelry pieces.

107. Quanah Alabaster

A more colorful alabaster here

See map on page 271.

Land type: Rolling plain with mesquite, woodlands, and grass prairies

GPS: 34.1640417 / -99.7407

Elevation: 1,688 feet

Best time of year: Spring, summer, fall

Land manager: Texas Department of Transportation

Material: Alabaster

Tools: Geological hammer, short handle rake, garden shovel, and spray bottle for small pieces. If you are after some sizable chunks, a sledgehammer, gads, crowbar, heavy duty gloves, respirator for those sensitive to dust, and chisel would be needed. Don't leave your upper body strength at home.

Vehicle type: Good road all the way to the site. 2-wheel drive is sufficient.

Precautions and restrictions: Be sure to pull completely off the pavement. The road is a bit narrow here. Use your warning flashers.

Accommodations: Copper Breaks State Park is about 13 miles from Quanah with a drive time of about 13 minutes. It offers a variety of camping experiences. The park does not have full hookup sites but does offer parking with electricity and water and campsites with water only. Besides the state park, there are a number of commercial RV parks and resorts in the area. Motels are located in the Quanah area.

SPECIAL ATTRACTIONS

Copper Breaks State Park's landscape is very scenic with mesquite- and grass-covered hills. It is a great place to do some bird watching for a number of species of ducks, roadrunners, meadowlarks, quail, doves, great blue herons, cardinals, flickers, bluebirds, kites, hawks, mockingbirds, a few species of owls, and many others.

Mammals also abound. On an early morning or late evening walk, you may spot mule deer, rabbits, raccoons, armadillos, opossums, bobcats, porcupines, and coyotes. A few species of frogs, toads, turtles, and lizards also call the park home.

Hiking is also a popular activity at the park. The trails can be used for walking or biking. The lake is stocked with rainbow trout and catfish. Loaner tackle is available.

FINDING THE SITE

Quanah is a city in and the county seat of Hardeman County. It is about 145 miles southeast of Amarillo, and it takes about 2 hours and 20 minutes to drive the distance. If you are approaching from the north: From the town of Quanah at the junction of US 287 and TX 6, drive south on TX 6 for 8.6 miles to a road cut with very large boulders on each side.

If you are approaching from the south: From the town of Crowell, at the junction of TX 6 and US 70 travel north on TX 6 for 12.6 miles. You will now be in the road cut with the large boulders.

ROCKHOUNDING

The soapstone here has a greenish tinge, and some of it appears to have crystals. Other pieces were more solid. The ones that contain crystals are located within an area where the stone eroded and formed toothlike structures.

108. South of Crowell Quartzite

The South of Crowell quartzite location

See map on page 271.

Land type: Rolling plain with mesquite, woodlands, and grass prairies

GPS: 33.8354307 / -99.5396187

Elevation: 1,379 feet

Best time of year: Spring, summer, fall

Land manager: Texas Department of Transportation

Material: Quartzite, flint

Tools: Geological hammer, short handle rake, garden shovel, spray bottle

Vehicle type: Good road all the way to the site. 2-wheel drive is sufficient.

Precautions and restrictions: Be sure to pull completely off the pavement. Use your warning flashers.

Accommodations: Copper Breaks State Park is about 9 miles north of Crowell with a drive time of less than 10 minutes. It offers a variety of camping experiences. The park does not have full hookup sites but does offer parking with electricity and water and campsites with water only. Besides the state park, there are a number of commercial RV parks and resorts in the area. Motels are located in the Quanah area.

SPECIAL ATTRACTIONS

Copper Breaks State Park's landscape is very scenic with mesquite- and grass-covered hills. It is a great place to do some bird watching for a number of species of ducks, roadrunners, meadowlarks, quail, doves, great blue herons, cardinals, flickers, bluebirds, kites, hawks, mockingbirds, a few species of owls, and many others.

Mammals also abound. On an early morning or late evening walk, you may spot mule deer, rabbits, raccoons, armadillos, opossums, bobcats, porcupines, and coyotes. A few species of frogs, toads, turtles, and lizards also call the park home.

Hiking is also a popular activity at the park. The trails can be used for walking or biking. The lake is stocked with rainbow trout and catfish. Loaner tackle is available.

FINDING THE SITE

Crowell is a city in Foard County. It is about 170 miles southeast of Amarillo with a drive time of 2 hours and 40 minutes. From Crowell at the junction of TX 6 and US 70, travel east on TX 70 for 8.3 miles to a junction with Texas Farm Road 267, travel south on this road for 8.3 miles, and turn southeast onto Texas Farm Road 1919. Drive 3.8 miles. You will be in a road cut of grassy hills.

Colorful quartzite from South of Crowell

ROCKHOUNDING

Quartzite is composed primarily of silicon dioxide. It is a hard, between 7 and 7.5 on the Mohs scale, and was originally sandstone that was then converted into a metamorphic rock primarily through heating and pressure usually related to tectonic compression. This site is littered with very colorful quartzite. Some gray to brown flint is also scattered around the area.

GLOSSARY

Agate: A form of chalcedony containing bands or mossy inclusions; often very colorful, but sometimes with either one color or very muted colors.

Aggregate: A mixture of different kinds of rocks or crystals.

Alabaster: A fine-grained variety of gypsum used widely for carving.

Amethyst: A gemstone of the quartz family, ranging in color from pale lilac to deep purple.

Ammonite: A cephalopod fossil curled like a ram's horn.

Apache tears: A kind of nodular obsidian (volcanic black glass). When polished, it is opaque to nearly translucent. The color ranges from red to brown to black.

Aquamarine: A form of beryl next in desirability to emerald; colors range from pale to deep blue or blue green.

Aragonite: A form of calcite that often forms in layers or bands and is sometimes mistaken for onyx.

Azurite: A blue copper carbonate often associated with malachite.

Baculite: A cephalopod fossil of the same family as the ammonite, but straight rather than curled.

Barite: Barium sulfate occurring in blue, green, brown, and red colors.

Beryl: Beryllium aluminum sulphate that is colorless in its pure form. Varieties include emerald, green; aquamarine, blue; morganite, pink; and heliodor, brown to golden yellow.

Brachiopod: A marine animal with two nearly symmetrical shells, but with one slightly larger than the other.

Cabbing: The act of creating a cabochon.

Cabochon (Cab): A common shape for a gem, usually with an elliptical perimeter and a domed top.

Calcite: Calcium carbonate that occurs in clear as well as white, brown, red, yellow, and blue crystals.

Caliche: A calcium carbonate mineral hardened with a natural cement that binds the materials together. It consists of gravel, sand, clay, silt or a combination of them. It occurs worldwide, in aridisol and mollisol soil orders—generally in arid or semiarid regions.

Candy rock: See picture rock.

Cephalopod: Free-swimming marine animal; ammonites and baculites are typical of cephalopods.

Chalcedony: A cryptocrystalline form of quartz in which the crystal structure is not visible to the naked eye; forms include agate, jasper, carnelian, sard, onyx, chrysoprase, sardonyx, rose, and flint.

Chert: See Flint.

Concretion: A cemented accumulation of mineral material; may contain pyrite, silica, calcite, or gypsum.

Country rock: The common rock surrounding a vein or other deposit of gemstones or minerals.

Cretaceous: The Cretaceous is the third and final period of the Mesozoic Era. It lasted about 79 million years in geological history, from about 145 to 66 million years ago.

Crinoid: One of hundreds of round stem-like echinoderms; usually only parts are found as fossils.

Crystal: A solid mineral having a regular geometric shape with flat faces or surfaces.

Dendrite: A mineral inclusion, usually manganese, in a rock that resembles the branching of a fern.

Dike: A wall of igneous rock surrounded by country rock.

Dumortierite: It is a colored, usually blue or purple, aluminium boro silicate mineral, $Al_7BO_3(SiO_4)_3O_3$. The crystals are orthorhombic. Typically it is a fibrous aggregate of slender prismatic crystals. The hardness is 7 on the Mohs scale and has a S.G. of around 3.3.

Epidote: Green crystal sometimes used as a gemstone, but more commonly collected for display.

Feldspar: The most abundant mineral in the Earth's crust; classified as orthoclase and plagioclase; among the most desired varieties are moonstone, sunstone, microcline, and labradorite.

Flint: Flint is a sedimentary rock consisting of microscopic, nearly undetectable (cryptocrystalline) crystals of the mineral quartz (SiO2).

Float: Gemstones or minerals that have been transported from their place of origin by water, erosion, or gravity.

Fluorite: A common mineral that occurs in colors of white, brown, purple, green, yellow, violet, and blue; sometimes faceted, but too soft to stand up to day-to-day wear as jewelry.

Fluorspar: A less pure and more granular form of fluorite.

Fortification agate: Agate with acutely banded corners that form a closed figure resembling a fort.

Fossils: Remains of plants, insects, or animals preserved in casts or molds.

Gad: A chisel or pointed iron or steel bar used for loosening ore or rock.

Gangue: Country rock, or other rock of no value, surrounding minerals or gemstones.

Garnet: A group of differently colored but chemically similar minerals. The group includes pyrope, red with brown; almandine, red with violet; spessartite, orange to red brown; grossular, yellow to copper brown; demantoid, emerald green; and uvarovite, emerald green.

Gem: A gemstone that has been prepared for use in jewelry.

Gemstone: Any precious or semiprecious stone that can be cut and/or polished and used in jewelry.

Geode: A hollow nodule or concretion, usually filled with crystal formations.

Granite: An igneous rock composed mostly of quartz and feldspar. It has high content of silica and alkali metal oxides that slowly cools and solidifies underground.

Gypsum: A hydrous calcium sulphate that occurs in white, colorless, gray, brown, red, and yellow; colorless variety is called selenite, and dense form is called alabaster.

Igneous: Rock formed by solidification or crystallization of lava.

Jasper: Opaque form of chalcedony, often with mossy inclusions or intertwining of various colors.

Lapidary: The art of forming and shaping gemstones; one who forms or shapes gemstones.

Lepidolite: Pink-to lilac-colored silicate mineral of the mica group.

Limonite: A term applied generally to a brownish iron hydroxide; often occurs as a pseudomorph after iron minerals such as pyrite.

Llanite: A grey or brown granite with blue quartz crystals. So far, it has only been found in Llano County, Texas.

Massive form: The form of a mineral in which the crystals are either very small or without any discernible definition.

Matrix: Material in which a mineral crystal or fossil is embedded.

Metamorphic: Preexisting rock changed by the action of pressure, chemical action, or heat; one of the three primary classifications of rock.

Mica: A group of sheet silicate minerals, major members of which are muscovite, biotite, phlogopite, lepidolite, and chlorite.

Micromount: A tiny mineral specimen intended for viewing under a microscope.

Monocot: Monocot is short for monocotyledons. They are grass and grass-like flowering plants (angiosperms), the seeds of which typically contain only one embryonic leaf, or cotyledon. Their circulatory systems are of multiple pairs of tubes as opposed to the xylem and phloem of other trees.

Onyx: A black-and-white-banded chalcedony; colored varieties sold in gift shops are either dyed onyx or a form of calcite or aragonite.

Opal: A silicon oxide closely related to chalcedony, but softer and containing water. Common opal is often dull and not suitable for jewelry, but some has a waxy texture and will cut and polish into nice cabochons; often replaces wood fibers in fossil wood and makes finely detailed samples. Precious opal is the type associated with fine jewelry and shows beautiful flashes of multicolored fire; often mistakenly called fire opal, but true fire opal is red and does not have the flashes of fire.

Orthorhombic: There are seven different crystal systems in crystallography. One is orthorhombic, which is a rectangular prism with a rectangular base. The height, width, and length all intersect at 90-degree angles.

Palm (petrified) wood: Is Palmoxylon. An extinct genus of palm trees that has been petrified. Found around the world.

Pegmatite: Coarse-grained igneous rock often the host for gemstones and minerals; usually found as smaller masses in large igneous formations.

Pelecypods: Bivalved mollusks with shells that meet evenly at the hinge; not symmetrical as in the brachiopods; oysters, clams, and mussels are typical pelecypods.

Petrification: The process by which silica or other minerals replace the cell structure of organic material.

Picture rock: A swirly patterned rhyolite used for jewelry and decorative pieces. Also called candy rock.

Porphyry: Rock containing crystals in a fine-grained mass.

Pseudomorph: A crystal with the geometric appearance of one mineral, but which has been chemically replaced with another mineral.

Pyrite: Iron sulfide or disulfide with a brassy yellow color; commonly called "fools' gold."

Quartz (Cryptocrystalline): Group that includes amethyst, aventurine, citrine, rose quartz, smoky quartz, and tiger eye.

Quartz (Macrocrystalline): Group that includes chalcedony, agate, jasper, onyx, chrysoprase, and sard.

Rhodochrosite: A manganese carbonate gemstone in colors from rose red to white with striping; sometimes forms as stalactites in caves.

Sard: A chalcedony that is somewhat translucent. It usually occurs as shades of gray or brown and is used for carved jewelry.

Sardonyx: Sard that is layered with different shades of material. Used to carve cameos and other pieces of jewelry.

Silicafied: A mineral or organic compound that has been replaced by silica.

Snake stick: A stick carried around when one anticipates encounters with snakes. It is used by rattling the brush ahead of you to chase away any reptiles.

Tailings: Waste material from mining or milling.

Zeolite: Any of various hydrous silicates that are analogous in composition to the feldspars and occur as secondary minerals in cavities of lavas.

SITE INDEX

ABOUT THE AUTHORS

Ruta Vaskys and Martin Freed are skilled writers and photographers who have been outdoor enthusiasts for many years with experience in trapping, collecting wild herbs, and rock identification. They spend most of their time living in Virginia.